Real Life
Has No
Expiration
Date

Real Life
Has No
Expiration
Date

Bruce & Stan

VINE
BOOKS

SERVANT PUBLICATIONS
ANN ARBOR, MICHIGAN

Vine Books is an imprint of Servant Publications especially designed to serve evangelical
Christians.

Scripture quotations are taken from the *Holy Bible*, New Living Translation, © 1996. Used
by permission of Tyndale House Publishers, Inc., Wheaton, Illinois 60189. All rights
reserved.

Published by Servant Publications
P.O. Box 8617
Ann Arbor, Michigan 48107

Cover design: Left Coast Design, Inc., Portland, Oregon

01 02 03 04 10 9 8 7 6 5 4 3 2

Printed in the United States of America
ISBN 1-56955-257-6

Library of Congress Cataloging-in-Publication Data

Bickel, Bruce, 1952–
    Real life has no expiration date: failure is not fatal / Bruce Bickel and Stan Jantz.
      p. cm.
    ISBN 1-56955-257-6 (alk. paper)
    1. Youth—Religious life. 2. Failure (Psychology)—Religious aspects—Christianity. I.
    Jantz, Stan, 1952– II. Title.

    BV4531.3 .B53 2001
    248.8'3—dc21

2001024067

Contents

Introduction

Michael's mother knocked at his bedroom door, and then stuck her head into the room and whispered:

Mom: Mikey, it's time to get up or you'll be late for school.
Michael: Ahh, Mom. I don't want to go to school. All the kids make fun of me, and all of the teachers ignore me.
Mom: Come on, now, Mikey. You have to get up and go to school.
Michael: But Mom, I'm no good at school. I'm such a loser. Everything always goes wrong. I'm a complete failure. Can't I just stay in bed and pretend to be sick today?
Mom: Michael, there are two very good reasons why you have to get out of bed and go to school today. First of all, you are forty-two years old. Secondly, you are the principal.

Most people can get out from under the covers at the beginning of each day, but that doesn't mean that they feel confident to tackle the circumstances of their lives. Their feelings of failure can be kept "undercover" even though their bed is made and they have changed out of their pajamas.

Are You Afflicted With Failure?

We live in a culture that abhors failure and praises success. We love winners and hate losers. Well, *hate* may be too strong a word. But we pity the losers and want to distance ourselves from them. In fact, our society gives the impression that there is only one thing worse than associating with a failure, and that is being one yourself.

It is surprising that our society has such a harsh attitude toward failure. Everyone has personally experienced it from time to time, but it seems to be spread around in different degrees. For some people, it is just an occasional occurrence; for others, it is a constant condition. How you feel about yourself (and how others react toward you) depends upon how bad you've been afflicted with it. Here's what we mean:

- **When your failures are just an occasional occurrence, it's like having a facial blemish:**

✓ You try your best to cover it up.

✓ Even though it still shows, it doesn't keep you from going out in public.

✓ Your friends can't help but notice it, but they are polite enough not to say anything about it.

✓ People who aren't your friends will point and snicker.

- **But when your failures are a constant condition, it seems like you are infected with the contemporary, cultural equivalent of leprosy:**

✓ Once you've got it, you are sure that you can never get rid of it.

✓ You are convinced that it's going to spread through your life until everything about you rots away.

✓ Everything you touch is tainted with it.

✓ No one wants to come near you, out of fear that some of what you've got will rub off on them. So, if you've got it, you're ostracized. Oh, the shame of it all.

But wait a minute! Failure doesn't have to be a fatal disease! And that is what this book is all about.

Take Bruce & Stan's Self-Diagnosis Failure Test

If the biggest failure in your life was choosing the wrong monogram for the floor mats in your Porsche, then put this book down. We aren't writing to you. You're the type that only has a blemish of a failure from time to time. You have no idea what we're going to be talking about.

This book is written for people who struggle with feelings of failure. It is for those people who are dissatisfied because they are falling short of certain expectations in one or more areas of their lives, and now they are beginning to lose the proper perspective about their entire lives. Is this you?

If you aren't sure, we have a simple test that you can administer to yourself (in the privacy of your own home or in the solitude between the bookstore stacks) to determine whether you should keep reading beyond this introduction.

You may be struggling with feelings of failure if ...

➤ Something good happens to someone else, and you immediately assume that it will never happen to you.

➤ You can easily recite a long list of things that you don't like about yourself, but you have never taken an inventory of your good qualities.

➤ Your vocabulary consists of more negative terms than positive ones.

➤ You watch *The Simpsons* television show and say: "I could never be as successful as Homer."

➤ You are constantly judging your accomplishments by those of others, but you always select people who have "done better than you" for the comparison.

➤ You intentionally schedule elective surgery to coincide with the date of your graduating class reunion so you'll have a legitimate excuse for missing it.

➤ You look in the mirror and never like what you see. (We are excluding the first look early in the morning. That should never be the subject of extended contemplation!)

➤ People ask, "How are you doing?" and your response sounds like it was uttered by Eeyore (the donkey from Winnie the Pooh who always sounds like he has overdosed on depressants).

➤ You've given up on your New Year's resolutions before the end of the Rose Parade.

➤ You go to your closet, and you always decide to wear sweatpants. (That's a universal sign in our culture that you have given up hope and are ready to disengage from society.)

If you can identify positively with any one of these categories, then you should skip immediately to Chapter 1 and don't stop reading until you reach the back cover (unless you are between the stacks in the bookstore, in which case you should proceed to the nearest cash register, consummate the purchase, and then go sit in your car and read until the dome light burns out).

We've Got Your Life Covered

We know you don't feel like a failure in *every* part of your life. You might be feeling inferior in just one specific area. That presents a bit of a problem for us, because you know what that one area is, but you haven't told us. So, we are going to cover the main areas of life where people feel failure-prone. The chances are that we'll hit your sore spot when we talk about:

⇒ *Family.* Perhaps you're worried that failure may be in your bloodline, and you're planning a transfusion.

⇒ *Friends.* Are you having difficulty establishing and maintaining friendships? Is your most meaningful daily contact with the cashier at your neighborhood Starbucks?

⇒ *Love & Romance.* Maybe you have stopped going to Thanksgiving dinner with the relatives because you don't want to be asked "the question" anymore.

⇒ *Career.* You wish you had a career that was going nowhere because it would be better than the one you've got that's going backward.

⇒ *Finances.* Are the directions of your financial life backward? Does your outgo exceed your income? Is your upkeep about to cause your downfall?

⇒ *Judgment.* Do you think you're a failure at making good choices? Are your natural instincts so bad that you've started to do just the opposite because it couldn't be any worse?

⇒ *Faith.* Maybe you are sick and tired of making promises to God that you never keep. Are you afraid that he is sick and tired of your broken promises, too?

You might not be struggling in all of these areas, but if you have failure feelings in at least one of them, then you might be susceptible to a failure affliction in the others.

This Book Isn't Really About Failure

Although we have used the "F" word twenty-one times already in this introduction, this book isn't really about failure. It is really a book about success. We want to help you change your way of thinking so that you start planning for success in the areas of your life where you are now obsessing about your failures. Here's how we look at it:

**Your failures can be stumbling blocks to success,
or they can be the starting blocks to success.
You determine the difference.**

If you are wondering whether we will be feeding you a bunch of psycho-babble, let us put you at ease. There will be none of that in this book. We won't give you any pop psychology because neither one of us is a psychologist. And we won't recommend any mystical meditation techniques such as *omphaloskepsis* [the contemplation of your bellybutton] because neither of us is flexible enough to assume those positions.

What we will focus on in each chapter is:

* *Attitude:* We'll help you think about your circumstances from a different point of view.

* *Application:* We'll go to the Bible and show you some real-life examples of failures who turned out to be successful.

* *Action:* We will give you some practical steps that you can put to use right away in your life.

We know that you probably have some very difficult circumstances in your life. We will not minimize the significance of those factors. But you shouldn't assume that they are insurmountable, or that you are incapable, or that your situation is irrevocable. So, get ready for some positive changes in your life. Failure is not fatal, and you don't have to spend all day in your pajamas (unless you are a sleepwear model for the Eddie Bauer catalogue).

PART ONE

Buried Beneath Failure

Success contains within it the germs of
failure, and the reverse is also true.

—Charles de Gaulle

Maybe you are anxious to examine the different areas of your life that you think are marred with failure flaws. Well, you are just going to have to wait until chapter three. You can't go there yet ... not until we get to what may be the root of the whole problem.

Before you can objectively examine your failures, you ought to make sure you are working with a correct definition of the term. That's what we'll be doing in this first chapter—coming to grips with what *failure* really means.

When properly understood, the concept of failure may not be as abhorrent to you, and the ramifications may not be as fatal as you had believed. But you'll never know unless you start off with a little linguistics.

After tackling the terminology, we'll ponder the perplexity of people's fear of failure in chapter two. On the anxiety scale, failure is right up there with: (1) public speaking, (2) snakes, and (3) showing up at work naked because you forgot to get dressed before you walked out of the house (which is a common fear although it would never happen because the outdoor breezes would alert you to your nudity as soon as you stepped outside).

After reading chapters one and two, you may have a different perspective about failure and may not be as fearful of it. (But you are on your own for public speaking and snakes.)

> **There are only two kinds of failures: the man who will do nothing he is told, and the man who will do nothing else.**

—Anonymous

CHAPTER 1

What Is Failure?

Most of your impressions about life were formed, or perhaps adjusted, since you have acquired at least a modicum of maturity. By that, we mean that you have rejected many of the misconceptions that you believed as a child.

- You have abandoned childish notions of the boogeyman;
- You no longer believe in Santa Claus;
- You know that stepping on a sidewalk crack won't break your mother's back; and
- You can make funny faces without any fear that your face will get stuck in that position.

We suspect, however, that one misconception from your childhood remains: Failure is bad ... very bad.

We know exactly how you came to adopt and adhere to this misconception. It was the fault of your grade-school teachers (with reinforcement from your parents). From the time that you turned in that very first homework assignment, you were subjected to a grading scale that went something like this:

Grade:	Stands for:	Really means:
A	Excellent	You've got this teacher pegged.
B	Good	Don't get too smug; there is still room for improvement.
C	Average	Average is really substandard, so this work is mediocre but not bad enough for punitive measures to be imposed.
D	Below Average	You're just hanging by a thread.
F	FAILURE	You are a big, fat Loser! Be prepared for a career where you'll be asking "Do you want to Super-size that?" for the rest of your life.

Did your teacher stop with just giving you a failing grade? Oh, no. To make the humiliation even more heinous, your teacher would emblazon that dreaded letter across the front of your paper in red ink. The public disgrace was intended as motivation for improvement in the future. (Our personal, unscientific studies have shown that "motivation by mortification" works on only about 50 percent of students; the rest drop out of school and spend the rest of their lives as street mimes.) Unfortunately, even the 50 percent that were motivated by this public humiliation learned another, more damaging lesson: all failure is shameful.

And Now a Word From Webster

Let's go to Webster for a definition (we're referring to the word guy, not the little kid from the 1980s sitcom). Here are a few common definitions of *failure* as found in Webster's New World College Dictionary:

- "The act of failing or the state or condition resulting from having failed." [Thanks, Webster. That really clears things up.]
- "Falling short."
- "A breakdown in operation or function."
- "Neglect or omission."

Those rather innocuous definitions don't make *failure* seem too bad. So what if you "fall short," slightly missing the mark? It's no big deal. How about an occasional breakdown? Nothing tragic about that. And who worries about a slight omission or a little neglect? That's just a part of life. Let's face it. If failure is nothing more than a mere oversight, then failure is nothing to fret about.

If that was the extent of society's perception of failure, you wouldn't be worried about it (and our publisher wouldn't have been interested in this book). But Webster, and society, make it personal by adding one more definition:

- "A person or a thing that fails."

Do you see what has happened? You (along with the rest of us) have been sucked into the failure vortex. Because we are all guilty of minor omissions—because we all fall short of the goal occasionally—that means we all *fail* from time to time. And, according to Webster, a person who fails is a *failure*. So much for self-esteem.

There it is! We have just identified the first major misconception about failure that impacts everything we will be talking about in the chapters that follow. And just in case you missed it, let us say it a bit more succinctly.

Major Misconception #1:
A person who fails is a failure.

Don't believe it. It isn't true.

**Failing doesn't automatically make you a failure.
Whether you are a failure or not
depends upon how you respond when you fail.**

A Successful Definition of Failure

There is a symbiotic relationship between success and failure. In some respects, the concepts are opposite and contradictory; but in other respects, they are interrelated and closely connected. Don't just take our word for it. Let's go back to Webster.

Webster uses references to success to define failure:

Fail: to be unsuccessful in obtaining a desired end
Failure: not succeeding in doing or becoming

Now, viewed from a superficial perspective, *success* is sometimes measured in terms of financial wealth or power or celebrity status. But setting aside the transitory and trivial connotations, self-help gurus and positive mental attitude advocates define *success* another way:

Success: the progressive realization of a worthwhile goal

Notice the elements that are included in such a definition:

- *Success involves progress.* One cannot be "successful" just by standing still. Success requires movement in a positive direction toward a goal.

- *Success involves the pursuit of something beneficial.* One cannot be considered "successful" by attaining goals that are without merit or value to yourself or others.

- *Success involves a predetermined target.* One cannot be successful by meandering randomly, without purpose or direction. Success implies hitting a target or attaining a goal.

Equally as important, notice what is *not* included in the definition:

- *Success is determined not by the destination, but by the journey to that destination.* Success isn't delayed until the goal is reached. Success is achieved as incremental progress toward the goal to be made.

- *Success is not dependent upon past accomplishments.* The question is not, "What have you achieved in the past?" Rather, success is defined by "Where are you going now?"

- *Success is not restricted by present circumstances.* Your situation can be bleak, but you can still be a success if you are making progress toward something better.

This definition of success (as progress toward a worthwhile goal) can be applied to any aspect of your life. For example, let's look at your career. If you spend the day asking, "Paper or plastic?" you might not have a high opinion of your occupational success. Yet, you are succeeding if you are spending a few evenings a week taking courses at the community college to earn a degree in accounting. Although you have not yet attained your goal of becoming a Certified Public Accountant, you are making progress toward that goal. You are doing what it takes to achieve that goal. That makes you successful.

We can hear what you're thinking. (Actually, we can't hear you at all. But we smelled something burning, so we figured you were cranking up the heat in your cranium.) You're thinking that the "grocery clerk/night school student" was a hypothetical situation designed to prove our point. You want to see how we respond if you tweak our example by supposing further that you fail the final exam in your Introduction to Accounting course. Dare we call your life "successful" if you have flunked the course and have to spend a few extra years bagging frozen peas and toilet paper?

Major Misconception #2:
Failing is always bad.

This gets us back to our definition of *failure*. Webster characterized failure as the absence of success. If success is movement toward a worthwhile goal, then failure occurs when you stop moving forward. You don't fail until you give up the effort. In our grocery clerk analogy, flunking the course does not mean you failed to reach your goal (preparing for your future career). What you do next determines whether or not you fail:

- You will fail if you abandon all hope and resign yourself to a lifetime of corralling runaway shopping carts; but

- You are still in the success mode if you make an appointment with the career planning counselor to find an occupation that doesn't involve numbers.

**Failing doesn't make you a failure.
Failing gives you an opportunity to
learn from your mistakes.**

Avoid Failure: Make a Mistake

Thomas Edison subscribed to this approach of refusing to characterize setbacks as failures. When he was chided for having so many failures in his attempt to invent an inexpensive electric light, he responded:

"I have not failed. I have just found 10,000 ways that will not work."

In other words, his path to success involved making many false starts and having many dead-end ideas. He was a success—because he knew how to learn from his many, many mistakes.

So, the next time you are tempted to get down on yourself for your *failures*, try changing your vocabulary a bit. Think of it not as a failure, but a *mistake*. The result is the same, but your attitude about what you have done may be different. Subconsciously, that little change of vocabulary can make a big difference. The kinds of things you say to yourself will differ drastically depending on whether you have failed or simply made a mistake:

When you have *failed*, you are thinking:
- Life is over.
- I'm doomed.
- I'm no good at anything.
- I can't face my friends.
- I'm locked in a downward spiral and can't pull out of it.

But when you have simply *made a mistake*, you are thinking:
- I'll try again.
- It's no big deal.
- Everybody makes mistakes.
- People might not even notice.
- I can learn a lesson from this, and I sure won't make that same mistake again.

Here's the point: You have been programmed to believe that failure is fatal. Mistakes, on the other hand, don't have that bad rap. Everybody knows that life goes on after a mistake.

The Greatest Mistake of All Time

We don't mean to imply that calling something a "mistake" (rather than a "failure") will lessen its severity. The consequences of your actions will be the same regardless of the nomenclature you attach to them. (You can even try to make it sound exotic by calling it *faux pas*—but it is still a screwup and you will have to deal with ramifications.)

The Bible provides us with the real-life account of the greatest mistake ever made. In fact, this single act by this one individual has the double distinction of being the world's greatest and first mistake. We are referring to Adam and his decision to disobey God's instructions.

You might be envious of celebrities who appear to live a privileged and a charmed life. Well, no one whose face has ever graced the cover of *People* magazine had a situation better than Adam's. When you analyze his circumstances, you've got to come to the conclusion that his life was perfect. In the days before his mistake, Adam had every guy's dream life:

Famous Mistake Makers

- In 1876, a young inventor named Alexander Graham Bell asked Mark Twain to invest $5,000 in Bell's new telephone company. Twain rejected Bell. Instead, Twain invested $250,000 in a venture to produce a typesetting machine, which failed. By 1894, Twain had declared bankruptcy.

- In 1926, two brothers pitched their idea about a cartoon movie featuring a rodent to MGM Studios. Louis B. Mayer rejected the proposal because he believed women in the audience would be frightened at the sight of a cartoon mouse. Walt and Roy Disney had to distribute their Mickey Mouse movies without the help of MGM.

- A skydiving instructor named Ivan McGuire jumped from the plane with a video camera so he could film his students as they descended. Unfortunately, he forgot that he wasn't wearing his parachute. (OK, not *every* mistake entitles you to a second chance.)

- For forty-seven days, the prestigious Museum of Modern Art in New York hung the *Le Bateau* painting by Henri Matisse upside down.

- Universal Studios turned down a young filmmaker named George Lucas when he proposed a project entitled *Star Wars*. Twentieth Century-Fox didn't make the same mistake.

- *There were no household chores.* The Garden of Eden was his home. He didn't have to worry about spending his Saturdays working on a list of household chores because he had no house. There were no plugged toilets or drippy faucets. Of course, he still had to mow the grass. (see Genesis 2:5).

- *No one cared if he wore the same thing every day.* Most guys would prefer to wear the same set of clothes every day until they needed to be fumigated. Of course, most of feminine society (especially wives) frown on this type of fashion impropriety. So, every day a guy must waste valuable time (that could be spent watching ESPN) wondering whether he can get away with wearing a shirt that he threw into the hamper two days ago. Adam had none of these problems.

- *He had an easy job.* OK, it was an important job, but it was an easy one: naming the animals. How hard could it be? He points at the parrot and says, "I name you 'the long-beaked squawker.'" And then he looks over at the cow and declares, "I dub thee 'the four-pronged white squirter.'"

- *He had the perfect marriage.* His was a marriage made in heaven. Literally. God handcrafted Eve especially for Adam. He suffered no angst wondering if she was *the right woman* for him. Plus, he had no in-law problems.

Despite all that he had going for him, Adam blew it when Eve offered him some of the forbidden fruit. There must have been a moment while he debated within himself whether he should follow God's instruction, or give in to his own self-will. Chomping on the forbidden fruit, he made a mistake that would affect all of humanity for all of time. In that split second of rebellion, Adam spoiled God's perfect creation by bringing the sin virus to the human race.

There were consequences to the defiant actions of Adam and Eve. Their close, intimate friendship with God was changed forever. They were expelled from the Garden of Eden. Their existence became a laborious one. Now they would know pain and sorrow and death.

Was Adam a failure because of this huge mistake? Well, he failed God; there is no doubt about that. But he didn't become forever useless. Here are two interesting points that are applicable to our analysis of failure and success:

- *Adam's failure was not a surprise to God.* God already had a plan in motion to respond to the effects of Adam's mistake. That plan included sending Jesus to Earth to be a sacrifice for the sins of Adam and the rest of the human race. Adam's failure did not disrupt God's plan.

- *God still had a role for Adam, even after his failure.* If you had been in God's place, you might have been tempted to strike Adam and Eve with a lightening bolt after their act of defiance. You know, obliterate them and start the world over. But God didn't consider Adam totally useless after his fruit fiasco. God continued to use Adam as the father of the human race. It was into Adam's bloodline that Jesus was born.

Those same two principles apply to your life:

- *Your failures do not catch God by surprise.* His plan for your life takes into account all the mistakes that you have made, and all of the ones you will make in the future. God intends for you to learn from your past mistakes. His plans for your future incorporate what you have experienced in the past.

- *God still has a role for you, despite your failures.* You are not dispensable to God. Quite the contrary. His love for you is not diminished by the mistakes he knows you will make during your lifetime. Your failures have not disqualified you or made you unsuitable for future successes. Your potential remains intact, and God intends for you to take advantage of this fact.

Like Adam, you are not going to escape the consequences of your poor choices. God won't rescue you from all of the negative ramifications that result from your bad judgment. Adam went on to have a long life, and you can, too. A literal reading of Genesis would suggest that Adam was only a few days old when he ate the forbidden fruit. He lived to be about 900 years old. That's a lot of living that took place after his colossal mistake. You probably won't get an extra 900 years, but you'll have enough time to recover from your mistakes and make progress toward your worthwhile goals.

If anyone deserved to be distraught over a mistake, it was Adam. While we are sure he regretted his momentary rebellion for all of those remaining 900 years, there is no indication that his one-time failure pushed him into a state of despondency. There is every indication that he enjoyed God's forgiveness and went on with his life. Those same options are available to you.

Of course, maybe it was easier for Adam. He never received an "F" on a homework assignment from a grade-school teacher, so he wasn't brainwashed with the misconception that failure is fatal and that failing is always bad. But in the final analysis, you may have the advantage. You've now been exposed to the concept that failures can be learning experiences that help you become successful. And you are able to enjoy certain comforts that were never available to Adam—like indoor plumbing and cotton clothing.

In this chapter we have tried to give you a broader definition of failure than the one you have been used to. We hope you're starting to see that it can be viewed as the foundation for success. But maybe you are still quaking in your boots at the thought of failure. Actually, your fear of failure may be more crippling than the failure itself. In the next chapter, we'll see if we can scare the fear out of you (or at least persuade you with logic and rationality).

> Let me assert my firm belief that
> the only thing we have to fear
> is fear itself.

—Franklin D. Roosevelt

CHAPTER 2

The Fear of Failure

Don't you love living in the Information Age? You've got instant access to almost every possible piece of useful knowledge and every ounce of useless trivia you could possibly want. However, there is a downside to having vast amounts of information at your fingertips. On any given day you can access any number of stories and news reports that don't exactly inspire confidence.

For example, we opened the newspaper this morning and read that "terrorists, drug lords, and foreign insurgents" have decided to use weapons of mass destruction, such as chemical or germ weapons, on the general population rather than confronting the superior power of the United States military. (We wondered if these delightful people had some kind of convention and took a vote.) That just makes your day, doesn't it?

Then we read that by the year 2015, AIDS will be a major problem in India, Southeast Asia, several countries of the former Soviet Union, and possibly China—in addition to Africa, where AIDS is already a tragedy of epic proportions. Boy, that gives you a warm, fuzzy feeling, doesn't it?

And then there's the everyday stuff that hits closer to home: crime and violence, economic recession, warning labels of every kind, exploding tires, and the constant threat that something you do every day—such as using your cell phone—could be slowly killing you. Kinda makes you want to call in sick—for the rest of your life!

When you think about it, there are plenty of reasons for us to fear leaving the house in the morning. But we do what we have to do and venture out of the safe confines of our humble abodes each day because we don't think anything bad can happen to us. Or if we are a teensy bit nervous, we take extra precautions, such as driving with both hands on the wheel. Or we may simply choose not to think about the dangers lurking out there in the real world. In other words, we use every psychological and emotional weapon in our arsenal to handle what could be a serious case of the jitters caused by ordinary fear.

A Different Kind of Fear

Yet there is a kind of fear that paralyzes us all from time to time—some of us more than others. It's an insidious fear that keeps us from venturing out, maybe not in a physical sense, but certainly in the area of our emotions. This fear isn't based on anything that truly exists, but rather on something that could happen if something that could go wrong actually *did* go wrong. We're talking, of course, about the fear of failure.

The fear of failure isn't something that is treated with pills or powders. As far as we can tell, there is no such thing as "Fear of Failures Anonymous." Nope, with this kind of fear you're completely on your own. That's the bad news. The good news is that every single person possesses this fear. All of us—even the most successful superachievers among us—are afraid of failing at some time or other.

So the question to ask yourself should not be: *Why am I afraid to fail?* Instead, your question should be: *What am I going to do about it?*

"Ordinary People – Extraordinary Fears"

Some people have fears that go beyond the normal fears everyone else experiences. These are called *phobias*, and they usually refer to specific objects or situations. Here are a few common phobias:

PHOBIA	FEARED OBJECT OR SITUATION
• Acrophobia	Heights
• Aerophobia	Flying
• Agoraphobia	Open spaces
• Aquaphobia	Water
• Mysophobia	Dirt and germs
• Xenophobia	Strangers
• Ochlophobia	Crowds
• Ophidophobia	Snakes
• Arachnophobia	Spiders

And then there are some very strange phobias (these are our personal favorites):

• Dimentophobia	Insanity
• Homilophobia	Sermons
• Phobophobia	Phobias

Finally, here are some phobias that don't actually exist, but we think they should:

• Algoraphobia	Al Gore
• Kingopopophobia	Michael Jackson
• Grossaphobia	Hair in the sink
• Hypophobia	Madonna

Admit It ... You're Afraid to Fail

It's OK to admit that you're afraid to fail. In fact, admitting it is the first step toward getting over the fear of failure. Anybody who tells you that they love to fail isn't being honest with you. Failure hurts. Failure is painful. Failure can be humiliating, especially when you fail in front of others. No doubt you can remember a time or two when you were a little kid, and you did something stupid, and the other kids laughed (or worse, laughed and pointed). That feeling of failure may be as real to you today as it was years ago.

Think back for a minute

Take a moment to describe a memory of failure that comes to you right now. Maybe it happened at school, or perhaps you were at home. Whatever the circumstance, briefly talk about one of your childhood failures:

_____

_____

_____

_____

_____

_____

_____

_____

The second step to getting over your fear of failure is realizing that great things are usually accomplished by people who are afraid to fail. How can we say this? It's simple. Any significant accomplishment carries with it an element of risk: the bigger the feat, the greater the chance that you're going to fail, and that's something most of us fear. Does this mean you shouldn't take chances, knowing you might fail? Not at all. As long as you remember that failure is not fatal, but rather opportunity to learn how to do something better, you can calculate the risk and move forward.

Sometimes the risk is *physical*, such as when—
1. Soldiers go to war.
2. Explorers set off in search of new places.
3. Daredevils attempt something no one else has done.

Sometimes the risk is *financial*, such as when you—
1. Change careers.
2. Start a new business.
3. Invest in a "can't miss" company.

Other times the risk is *emotional*, such as when you—
1. Give a speech.
2. Make a new friend.
3. Assert yourself.

Persistence Pays Off: A Historical Perspective

One of the greatest leaders in history was also one of the greatest failures. The next time you feel like giving up, read this list of milestones in the life of Abraham Lincoln:

	Age
Failed in business	22
Ran for the legislature and lost	23
Failed in business again	24
Elected to the legislature	25
Sweetheart died	26
Suffered a nervous breakdown	27
Ran for speaker and lost	29
Ran for elector and lost	31
Ran for Congress and lost	34
Elected to Congress	37
Lost his seat in Congress	39
Ran for the Senate and lost	46
Ran as vice president and lost	47
Ran for Senate again and lost	49
Elected president of the United States	51

Feel the Fear

In her book, *Feel the Fear and Do It Anyway*, Susan Jeffers writes about three levels of fear.

"Level 1" fears come from external situations, such as illness, aging, or being alone. These are things many people worry about, even though they have little or no control over them.

"Level 2" fears involve your inner state of mind (for example, fear of failure). This type of fear involves the ego and also includes the fear of rejection, disapproval, and even success—all of which are closely related to failure.

Dr. Jeffers calls the "Level 3" fear the "I can't handle it" fear. "At the bottom of every one of your fears is simply the fear that you can't handle whatever life may bring you."

Think about this for a minute. Dr. Jeffers isn't saying—and neither are we—that the fear of failure, rejection, disapproval, or even success isn't real. Quite the opposite. The fear can be so real that it can keep you from accomplishing great things—or anything at all! Do you feel stuck in a dead-end job? It may be that you're afraid to change careers because you think you might fail at something you've never done before. Are you in a relationship that has your stomach in knots? It may be that you're afraid to assert yourself because you believe the other person may reject you. Is there something you've always dreamed of doing—maybe writing a book, composing a song, or painting a picture—but you don't dare express yourself because others may not approve?

It's bad enough that the fear of failure can immobilize you. Even worse, the fear of failure can keep you from doing something that may have great value to you and others. It's a double whammy! Nobody wants to live with regrets. None of us looks forward to the day at the end of our lives when we lament, "If only." And yet, it isn't the dumb stuff that you will surely regret the most. It's the significant stuff you *didn't* attempt—simply because you were afraid to fail.

Five Truths About Fear

Dr. Susan Jeffers lists these helpful principles about fear in her book, *Feel the Fear and Do It Anyway.*

1. *Your fear will never go away as long as you allow it to continue to grow.*
2. *The only way to get rid of your fear of doing something is ... to go out and do it. Similarly, the only way to feel better about yourself is to go out ... and do it.*
3. *Remember, everyone experiences fear whenever they're in unfamiliar territory.*
4. *Pushing through fear is less frightening than living with feelings of helplessness.*

Who Do We Think We Are?

Not long ago we were asked to write a book based on a major motion picture. We were flabbergasted. We were a couple of no-name, hack authors (this was before we became fairly well-known hack authors), and now someone wanted us to get involved with a big Hollywood production. It didn't take us five seconds to say yes. Then the reality of the project hit us and we got weak in the knees.

Our book was going to be one of several different titles based on *The Prince of Egypt,* a full-blown animated feature from DreamWorks on the life of Moses (he was the Prince of Egypt) and the Exodus. Our assignment was to write fourteen chapters based on the first fourteen chapters of the book of Exodus.

There were a few qualifications. First, the book had to appeal to children ages ten to fourteen (we had never written a book for children before). Second, the book was going to be based on notes and insights from Charles R. Swindoll (he just happens to be one of the best-selling Christian authors of all time). And third, the book had to be faithful to the film script (this meant that the head honchos at DreamWorks would need to give their final approval).

After we had agreed to write the book, we realized that every word would be scrutinized by editors (we were used to that), a major author (that was new), and a bunch of film people (gulp). Suddenly we got very nervous. What if we couldn't write for kids? What if Dr. Swindoll thought we were a couple of nincompoops? What if the creative types at DreamWorks flushed us down the Hollywood toilet? Our reputation with publishers (such as it was) could be damaged. Our career as a writing team (such as it was) could be ruined. Worse, there was a great possibility that we would never work in Hollywood again. (OK, so that was a stretch, since the likelihood of another opportunity like this one was remote indeed, but you get the point. Often our fears are based on fantasies rather than fact.) We sank to that "Level 3" fear. Instead of saying, "We can handle this," we said to ourselves, "Who do we think we are?"

Well, there's a happy ending to this story. We took Dr. Jeffers' advice and went out there and did it. Even though we were in unfamiliar territory, our desire to grow as writers was greater than our fear. So we wrote the book, everyone signed off, and it turned out to be an enriching experience. While we haven't received any offers to script a screenplay or anything like that, our work with the publisher led to another book for children ages ten to fourteen.

When Fear Leads to Failure

The fear of failure can keep you from moving forward, and sometimes fear can bring about failure. In their book *Leaders,* Warren Bennis and Burt Nanus tell the story of Karl Wallenda, patriarch of the famous Flying Wallenda tightrope and aerial artists. Karl Wallenda fell to his death while trying to walk a highwire in San Juan, Puerto Rico, in 1978. He had performed such feats hundreds of times before, each time overcoming his fear of failure.

Wallenda's wife recalled that every other time he had performed this feat he had concentrated on succeeding. For his final performance, he had changed his strategy: All he could talk about was not falling.

While his death was a tragedy, to those who knew the Great Wallenda, it was not a mystery. Bennis and Nanus observed: "It became increasingly clear that when Karl Wallenda poured his energies into not falling rather than walking the tightrope, he was virtually destined to fail."

The Prince of Egypt Was a Big Failure

Our experience with *The Prince of Egypt* (it's a wonderful film, by the way, and we strongly suggest that you see it in video or DVD) taught us another valuable lesson, and it directly relates to this chapter on the fear of failure. You see, Moses was one of the greatest failures of all time, yet he became one of the greatest heroes of all time—all because he trusted God and overcame his fear of failure. (If you know the story of Moses and the Exodus, please bear with us as we give you a thumbnail sketch of the dramatic events of Exodus 1-14.)

Our story opens with the nation of Israel enslaved by the Pharaoh of Egypt. There are more than two million adult Israelites living in Egypt, and most of them are forced to build cities and monuments under the harshest of conditions. The Pharaoh was concerned that the Israelites were growing too numerous, so he decreed that all the male Hebrew babies should be killed.

One particular Hebrew mother decided to protect her infant son by sending him down the river in a basket. By God's providence, the baby was discovered by Pharaoh's daughter, who brought him to the king's palace and raised him as one of Pharaoh's own sons. She named him Moses, which means "deliverer" in Hebrew. Moses was educated in the finest schools and given all the privileges of royalty. Yet he was troubled by the brutality of the Egyptian taskmasters, who drove the Hebrews—his people—mercilessly. In a fit of rage, Moses killed an Egyptian who was beating a Hebrew man.

Moses was forced to flee to the wilderness, where a Hebrew family took him in. He married into the family and lived with them for many years as a simple shepherd, far from his failure as the Prince of Egypt. Meanwhile, the Israeli slaves continued to suffer and they cried out to God for help. God heard their cries and announced a plan to deliver his people, only he didn't broadcast his plan to the masses. He told only one person—Moses.

If you've seen *The Prince of Egypt* or *The Ten Commandments* (the movie that made Charleton Heston famous)—or you just know your Bible—then you know how the story goes. Moses went back to Egypt and confronted Pharaoh, who refused to let God's people go. After a series of plagues that devastated the land and people of Egypt, Pharaoh finally relented, only to change his mind and pursue the nation of Israel right up to the Red Sea, where the Egyptian army faced a miraculous and rather resounding defeat. We won't go into those details, but we do want to back up and tell you about the way God convinced Moses to overcome his fear of failure so he could accomplish something truly significant.

Failure seldom stops you; what stops you is the fear of failure.

—Jack Lemmon

Failure's Five Excuses

The conversation between God (who spoke from a burning bush) and Moses is one of the greatest examples of one person trying to avoid doing something because he was afraid to fail. Thankfully, it is also one of the greatest lessons ever about the way to overcome the fear of failure. Before we go on to tell you about this dialogue, we encourage you to read it for yourself in Exodus, chapters 3 and 4. Go ahead, we'll wait.

OK, now that you're back, see if you came to the same conclusions we did (only we must warn you, we had help from Dr. Swindoll). This dramatic story begins when God tells the shepherd Moses (formerly known as Prince) to go back to the place of his birth in order to lead God's people out of Egypt. It was a tall order, but this was God speaking (and from a fiery shrub to boot).

How could Moses say no? Well, he did—five different times and in five different ways. Moses thought he was a failure and therefore unworthy, incapable, and just plain unwilling to take up the challenge, but God had a better idea. He patiently responded to each of Moses' excuses until Moses ran out. He convinced Moses that it didn't matter what Moses could or couldn't do—only what God was able to do.

Here are Moses' five excuses along with God's five responses from Exodus 3 and 4. See if you identify with these (we certainly can):

The Excuse	What It Meant	God's Response
"Who am I?" (3:11)	"I'm a failure, remember?"	"I will be with you." (3:12)
"They won't believe me." (3:13)	"I don't trust you enough."	"Tell them I have sent you." (3:14)
"They won't do what I tell them." (4:1)	"I lack confidence."	"Perform this sign." (4:5)
"I'm just not a good speaker." (4:10)	"I don't have the skills."	"Who makes mouths?" (4:11)
"Please send someone else." (4:13)	"I just don't want to do it."	"I will help you." (4:15)

There are some very powerful principles at work in this little dialogue. The first one goes back to a statement we made earlier in this chapter: *The greatest accomplishments come from people who are afraid to fail.* When Moses eventually overcame his fear of failure and accepted the task at hand, his life and his work took on tremendous importance. If Moses had said no to God's final offer, God would have found someone else to do the job (he always does). And Moses would have remained in the wilderness as a shepherd, living out his days in insignificance.

What about you? Has God asked you to do something great? Has he gifted you to impact the lives of others? Has he prepared you to accomplish something great? We don't know the specific answers to these questions, but we know the general answer to all three. Are you ready? The answer is *yes.* God has asked you to do something great. He has blessed you with gifts and talents so you can influence others. And he has prepared you (and will continue to prepare you) to accomplish things far beyond your wildest dreams. That much we know. What we don't know—and only you can answer this— is whether you are willing to overcome your fears in order to do what God wants you to do.

What God Will Do for You

You may be scratching your head, wondering how we can know with such certainty that God wants you to do something great. Actually that's easy to answer, because the Bible is very clear that God has a purpose for every person who follows him. Jesus articulated this purpose very clearly right before he left the earth: *"Go into all the world and preach the Good News to everyone, everywhere"* (Mark 16:15).

Of course, this purpose is very clear, but it's also fairly general. That is, where you go and how you do it is going to be an individual thing. There's no set pattern that says, "OK, everyone whose last name ends in 'A' goes to Asia, and everyone whose last name ends in 'B' goes to Borneo," and so forth. We believe that God has something unique for each of us to do, because each of us is created uniquely by God.

Already we're sensing some butterflies out there (someone once said that it's all right to have butterflies in your stomach, as long as they're flying in formation). So we want to review God's responses to Moses and put them in some kind of practical order for you. This is what God did for Moses, and he promises to do the same for you:

1. **God will be *patient* with you.** When you read Exodus 3-4, one of the things you realize is that God was incredibly patient with Moses. He answered each excuse with a reasoned response. The apostle Peter wrote: "He is being patient for your sake. He is giving more time for everyone to repent" (2 Peter 3:9). When you repent, it means you change direction. God is waiting for you to turn from fear of failure to follow him fully.

2. **God will give you his *presence*.** When Moses reminded God that he was a failure, God assured Moses that he would not be alone. He promises the same to us. You may fail, but you will not be a failure if God is with you.

3. **God will be with you in *person*.** A lot of people today view God as some kind of impersonal "force" that exists only because we invented it.

Others claim that the best way to find God is to draw upon the "spirit" within you. These beliefs are human centered. We must understand— as Moses did—that God is a personal being who exists apart from us. He is infinite, eternal, all-powerful, all-knowing, and completely holy. When Moses asked God to describe himself, God said: "I Am the One who always is" (Exodus 3:14). There is none like God. He created the universe and everything in it, and he cares about each of us.

4. **God will give you** *power.* When you lack confidence, as Moses did, remember that God will give you the ability to get things done. This doesn't mean you don't have to practice or prepare (sometimes for a long time). God has already given you gifts and abilities, and he expects you to use them for his glory. But God is always ready to supplement your abilities with his power.

5. **God will give you a** *purpose.* God promised Moses that he would tell him what to say. Do you lack direction in your life? Would you love to have some kind of powerful purpose? Trust God to give you his purpose. It may come through the Bible, or through the caring words of a trusted friend, or the wise counsel of a mentor. You may be inspired though a class at school or a course of study. God may even give you a vision that no one else can see. However it comes, God has a purpose for you.

6. **God will give you a** *plan.* Moses worried that his speaking ability (or lack thereof) would lead to his failure. No problem. God promised to provide someone to come alongside and help him deliver God's message. We can identify with this, because neither one of us feels talented enough or knowledgeable enough to write a book like this. But between us, we feel confident enough to get the job done. There's strength in numbers, even if it's just you and one other person.

The Antidote to Fear Is Faith

Often we live in fear because we don't know what's going to happen. The way to overcome uncertainty about the future is to have faith. This isn't a blind faith, or a wishing faith. The God of the Bible promises to give us everything we need to succeed, even if we can't see what's ahead. "What is faith? It is the confident assurance that what we hope for is going to happen. It is the evidence of things we cannot yet see" (Hebrews 11:1-2). It isn't God who causes our fears. To the contrary: "God has not given us a spirit of fear and timidity, but of power, love, and self-discipline" (2 Timothy 1:7).

What to Do Next

Knowing all of this stuff and knowing what to do next are two different things. It's not like you can turn off the fear and turn on the faith. Even Moses had to return to his home and talk things over with Jethro, his father-in-law (see Exodus 4:18). He did the right thing. If you feel God has spoken to you and given you a purpose and a plan, don't just run out there blindly and try to succeed by yourself, like Don Quixote charging a windmill. Find someone wiser and older—someone known for spiritual maturity—and talk things over.

Fear is a funny thing. It can go away for a while, but then it can return like a snakebite and hit you when you least expect it. You need people around you who can help you deal with your fears. Most of all you need to stay close to God by praying and reading his Word.

Moses certainly took this path after the failures in his life. Rather than denying that he had failed, Moses became teachable and obedient. Moses had been the prince of Egypt, and then he became a nobody. When he accepted God's challenge to return to Egypt, he did so as a servant rather than a prince. He also learned to depend on God, especially when the days got dark and it looked like he would fail once again.

Our problem isn't that we've failed. Our problem is that we haven't failed enough. We haven't been brought low enough to learn what God wants us to learn.

—Chuck Swindoll

From Failure to Success

We'd like to close this chapter with some words of advice from Dr. Robert Schuller, the old master of "possibility thinking." In his book, *You Can Become the Person You Want to Be,* Dr. Schuller gives nine tips for "stopping your fears before they stop you." According to Schuller, you need to overcome the fear of failure before you can start on the road to success.

1. *Expose your fear of failure to the light of truth.* Schuller explains that you are not really afraid of failure. What you fear is the embarrassment caused by failure. Get over it. Realize that "honest failure is no disgrace—lack of faith is the real shame."
2. *Realize that fear of failure does not promote or protect self-respect.* In fact, it does just the opposite. Fear of failure reduces your self-confidence and promotes the "what if" mentality.
3. *Remind yourself that there's no progress without risk.* Schuller writes: "Not until you have a failure can you be sure you aimed high enough. Success is making the most of the opportunity God has given you. Failure is failing to make the most of the gifts and lifts God offers you."
4. *Remind yourself that if you allow your fear to control you, you will live a dull, boring life.* Schuller isn't advocating living a risky life, but it's almost worse to live a life with no risk at all.
5. *Forget about being perfect.* Many people live in fear because they think they will fail if they can't do something perfectly. Guess what? Nobody can. The only thing you can do perfectly is nothing.
6. *Realize that failure is never final and total.* This is a big one. It's

almost impossible to succeed without first failing.

7. *Real failure is to fail as a person.* Most of us worry about failing at things we *do* rather than succeeding at who we *are.*

8. *Remove yourself from people who feed your fears.* If you hang around negative people, you will pick up their negative thoughts and behavior. You've heard the expression, "Starve a fever." Make it a point to starve your fears.

9. *Join the N.F.A. Club.* That's what Schuller calls the "Never Fear Again Club." You get into this club by developing "a strong personal faith in God."

In the whole, worded, sorry spectacle of human fears, none is more destructive and defeating than fear of failure. Eject this fear out of your life.

—Robert Schuller

PART TWO

Moving Beyond Failure

When I was young, I observed that nine
out of every ten things I did were failures,
so I did ten times more work.

—George Bernard Shaw

In Part One we discussed failure in a rather generic way. We didn't get too personal with you. Well, this isn't Part One anymore. Get ready for some real life.

In the next seven chapters, we're going to probe into some intimate areas of your life. We'll be discussing aspects of failure in:

- Your family relationships
- Your friendships
- Your love life
- Your career prospects
- Your finances
- Your common sense
- Your religious faith

You can't get much more intimate than that. But don't worry. We aren't trying to pry, or wanting to invade your privacy. As a matter of fact, we'll just raise the issue of failure—and success—in these areas. You can apply the concepts to your own situation and keep them secret from us. We won't even peek.

Someone once said that failure is the path of least persistence. It happens when you don't make the effort to change. In the chapters that follow, you'll have a chance to examine specific areas of your life. We'll help you consider whether any changes are appropriate, but you'll have to supply the effort on your own.

> Happy families are all alike;
> every unhappy family is
> unhappy in its own way.

—Leo Tolstoy

CHAPTER 3

When Failure Runs in the Family

We were working on the final drafts of this book on Saturday, January 20, 2001. That date has significance beyond the fact that it was the day Bruce finally took down the Christmas decorations at his house (despite requests from his wife to do so for the preceding twenty-five days). The real significant event of the day was the inauguration of George W. Bush as the 43rd President of the United States.

Regardless of anyone's political persuasions or proclivities, the event was remarkable from a *family* perspective. Within a radius of fifteen feet on the platform on the Capitol steps sat:

- the father, George Bush, who has served as a U.S. ambassador, head of the CIA, vice president, and president;
- the brother, Jeb Bush, the current governor of Florida; and
- the man of the hour, Dubya, who had transitioned from governor of Texas to president of the United States.

The influence of George and Barbara Bush on their sons was a subject of lengthy discussion and analysis by the television commentators (due in part to the length of the boring inaugural parade). George W. also acknowledged his parents' influence in his first official speech as president. He stated that the inaugural ceremony was not only a tribute to the peaceful transition of leadership in our country, but also "a tribute to my parents, who instilled values and gave unconditional love."

One thing was clear. Those Bush boys were raised in a family that was programmed for success. It was a family that had everything going for it. By all accounts, the Bush family consistently displayed love, commitment, and gentleness toward each other. And it certainly didn't hurt to be able to add wealth, power, privilege, and intelligence to the mix. The gene pool even produced some handsome men and attractive women.

But what about the rest of us? While the Bush family had a father who lived in the White House, many families have a father who doesn't live in their house at all, or who is pretty much an absent member of the household. And the Bush family attended fancy diplomatic dinners, while other families spend suppertime yelling at each other in a very undiplomatic fashion, or they never eat together at all. Everyone just sort of fends for himself (or herself). And while the Bush family traditions are featured in a cover story of *Good Housekeeping* magazine, the activities of some of the members of other families may be recorded on police rap sheets.

Let's face it. Many people endure family relationships and circumstances that make life difficult:

- Divorce has destroyed about half of all marriages, and the other half often experience friction and unhappiness.

- Single parents are faced with the struggles of multitasking all family leadership roles; they often feel inadequate, and many children often feel overlooked.

- The members of extended family are often sources of additional irritation. There are overbearing parents and intrusive in-laws. And let's not forget the adult siblings who subscribe to a family motto of: "All for one, and I'm the one."

What are your prospects for the future if you look at the members of your family and the only common resemblance you see is failure? Is it possible that failure runs in the bloodline and you are genetically doomed to a futile and frustrating life? Even if you want to break from family tradition and make a success of your life, has your heritage left you:

- *Unloved?* Friends come and go, but family is forever. That's not a very promising prospect if you're stuck within a family that shows hostility instead of affection. Will the love that bonds other families always be unavailable to you?

- *Unprepared?* How can you break a cycle of family instability if you have never had an appropriate role model? Are you ill-equipped to make your own family successful because you didn't have appropriate training when you were a child?

- *Unable?* You might be the only one in your entire family who is trying to repair the broken relationships. Is it possible for one person to fight against the momentum of hostility and antagonism? If it is going to be futile in the end, is it even worth the effort?

If we have just described your family, and if you have ever asked yourself any of these questions, then this chapter is for you. If you feel like chopping off a few branches of your family tree, then keep on reading. We've got exactly what you need: good news. Regardless of your family experience, there is a way for you to experience a loving family. You are not doomed to repeat the mistakes of your predecessors; and your efforts, even if ridiculed by the rest of your family, will make a difference.

Family Traits

At the outset, let's discuss what it means to have a family that is stuck in the failure mode. It is not a matter of finances. (There are families who are very happy living in a single-wide mobile home and driving a 1973 Pinto, and there are those with a penthouse and Porsche who are miserable.)

Education, in and of itself, is not the solution, either. Boarding school graduates don't necessarily make better family members than those released from reform school.

And it is not a matter of reputation. A good reputation may simply mean that you don't have inquisitive neighbors.

The traits that distinguish successful families from failing families are intangible qualities. Successful families exhibit qualities in their relationships with each other that foster a sense of togetherness. Failing families lack such cohesive qualities. While there is no single, exhaustive, or definitive list of such qualities, they are easy to identify. Just compare a family that is falling apart with one that is holding together. Let's take a look at a few of those qualities now.

A Sense of Protection

Norm (the frequent bar patron on the sitcom *Cheers*) said it best: "It's a dog-eat-dog world out there, and I feel like I'm wearing Alpo underwear." Norm (or his scriptwriter) was correct: Life can be pretty brutal, and you can get knocked around. It happens at work, or at school, or in other social settings. People are mean to each other. They can be bitter and abusive. There should be one place where you can go where you don't have to worry about people being hostile toward you. That place should be your home.

Successful families make their home a place of sanctuary. In these households, you don't have to keep your guard up. You aren't worried about being betrayed or attacked. You can relax, knowing that everyone is on your side.

That's not true in failing families. In these households, there is often more hostility than on the streets. That's why the members of failing families often prefer to be anywhere else than at home.

Affection

It takes more than tranquility to make a family successful. There need to be positive displays of affection.

- A clinical study at UCLA determined that men and women require eight to ten meaningful touches each day to maintain optimal emotional and physical health.

• Researchers at Purdue University asked the librarians to touch the hands of some of the students as they handed back their library cards, and to refrain from touching others in the same procedure. The survey results showed that those who had been touched reported far greater positive feelings about the library and the librarians. Those who were untouched were less impressed.

The physical contact in failing families is often nonexistent or consists of a slap on the side of the face. Successful families, on the other hand, employ the hugging technique.

**Successful families make physical contact.
It doesn't leave a mark,
but it makes a lasting impression.**

A Spirit of Forgiveness
Many families have been blown apart because the members hold grudges against each other. As time goes on, the resentment builds. What might have been a minor offense becomes a source of anger and hatred.

Failing families can't forgive each other. They often say it is a matter of principle, but it is usually just a matter of pride and stubbornness. And if one reluctantly apologizes and the other accepts it begrudgingly, both still keep score of who did what to whom. Successful families know that forgiving also requires mentally setting aside any record of wrongdoing.

Shared Priorities
A family lacks unity when each member has his or her own agenda and priorities. A shared sense of purpose brings a family together. Although family members may differ in their abilities and interests, they can share values. The greatest way to solidify a family is to share a common spiritual faith.

> In failing families, everyone marches
> to the beat of his own drum.
> In successful families, everyone plays
> a different instrument, but they march together.

Discipline

The mere mention of the word *discipline* brings to mind torture strategies designed to curb childhood disobedience. (In some families, it is "the belt" or the wooden "spanking spoon." In other families it is unplugging the Sony PlayStation.) Certainly child discipline is important. You don't want the kids to tear up the house. But that's not the kind of discipline we are talking about. We are referring to the self-discipline that the adults need so they don't break up the home.

Failing families are led by adults who don't have the self-discipline to make family a priority. Maybe they spend too much time at work, or perhaps they don't want to give up their own free time. Some choose to spend money on their hobbies rather than for the benefit of the entire family.

Successful families are led by adults who have learned the discipline of self-sacrifice. They are willing to forgo their own preferences for the good of the entire family.

What We Have Here Is a Failure to Communicate

Perhaps the greatest difference between failing families and successful ones has to do with the communication between the family members. All households have talking, but that doesn't mean that there is meaningful conversation.

- Failing families talk at each other. Successful families talk with each other.
- Failing families hear each other. Successful families listen to each other.

The difference is all about the respect that you give to one another. Significant conversations happen only when you regard others comments to be as important as your own.

In his book, *God's Man in the Family*, author Floyd McClung, Jr. emphasizes seven communication styles that actually hinder good communication between family members. He refers to them as being "deadly" because they cause family members to grow apart from one another. In other words, they cause failure in the family. Here is his list:

1. *The commander-in-chief.* This person loves to shout orders and be in charge. Any questions or suggestions or conflicting opinions are viewed as a sign of disloyalty.

2. *The moralist.* Conversations with this individual are always evaluated according to his or her personal standard of right and wrong. The value of your comments depends upon how you measure up against the moral authority.

3. *The know-it-all.* Don't even bother talking with these types. They don't listen. Why should they? You don't know anything. But since they know everything, they'll be glad to give you a lecture on the subject (any subject).

4. *The judge.* This person is more attentive than the other three because he or she is interested in hearing the different opinions and then making a definitive pronouncement. But you had better get your opinion in before the judge speaks. Once the judge's verdict is announced, there is no appeal.

5. *The critic.* Ridicule and sarcasm are the communication tools used in this style. The critics' own opinions are not even that important to them. Their primary purpose is to discredit the opinions of others. "What a stupid thing to say!" is a favorite phrase.

6. *The psychologist.* This person will probe you uncomfortably for your feelings. The analysis is usually clinical and based on curiosity; there is usually no personal concern for you. (How do you feel about that?)

7. *The consoler.* This one is all talk and no action. As you spill your guts about a personal crisis, you'll get a nod of the head and maybe a pat on your back. You'll hear, "Everything will be all right," but the consoler stops there. There is no follow-through to aid you in any way.

Members of failing families tend to communicate in one of two ways: either they talk too much, or they listen too little.

There Is No "Fun" in Dysfunctional

An article in *Focus on the Family* magazine calculated and categorized the time spent by the average person during a 70-year lifetime. The breakdown went like this:

- 23 years sleeping
- 16 years in school and at work
- 8 years watching television
- 6 years eating
- 6 years commuting
- 4.5 years in leisure activities
- 4 years sick
- 2 years getting dressed
- 0.5 years in church

That list is rather depressing, when you think about it. Only about 6.4 percent of your life is spent in leisure activities (away from the TV), just having fun. That's only a slightly larger portion of your life than that you'll spend being sick.

The "fun time" percentage is even lower in failing families. They simply don't have fun together. There is little laughter in the home of failing families.

The importance of laughter in life has been scientifically documented. Medical journals have reported that laughter can have a healing and beneficial effect on illness. Studies have shown that when hospital wards are visited by clowns (we're talking about the circus performers, not the attorneys from the HMO's), the patients—both children and adults—recover more quickly from surgery. Even Hollywood has emphasized the point with *Patch Adams*, the true-life story starring Robin Williams as a physician who employed laughter as part of his bedside manner.

Successful families reinforce their relationships when they spend time having fun together. Since there is affection among the family members, they actually enjoy each other's company. The ability to laugh and play with each other creates positive memories. Failing families have little of this. Their relationships haven't developed to the point where they enjoy being with each other; as they become more distant and isolated from each other, the relationship continues to deteriorate.

Failure Is Not Hereditary

If you were raised in a family that has failure traits, don't go shrieking into the street in the mistaken belief that you are genetically doomed and must have a hysterectomy or vasectomy to avoid subjecting offspring to the same fate. Or, if you are in a family situation now that has failure features on everyone's face, don't feel compelled to join a crew on the Alaskan pipeline as a way of escaping them.

Even though they are highly contagious, the traits of failing families are not hereditary. You won't inherit them just because you share the same bloodline as your relatives. You can take some deliberate steps to avoid repeating mistakes that plagued your ancestors. A proactive approach on your part may rescue you and bring relief to others in your family as well.

Compensating for Your Family's Failures

If you weren't raised in a caring and loving family environment, you may be at a bit of a disadvantage (but we aren't telling you anything you don't already know). You may be missing the care and support that comes from a close-knit family, and it may be a little more difficult for you to create that type of setting as an adult in your own family because you don't have the experience from which to build. But don't despair. A successful family environment is available to you from another source.

Your Spiritual Parentage

God is the perfect father. Have you ever thought of him that way? The Bible describes our relationship with God in familial terms. He is our *heavenly Father*, and we are his *children*. He is just the kind of father you have always wanted and needed.

- He is trustworthy. (see Deuteronomy 7:9)
- He is gracious and merciful. (see Nehemiah 9:31)
- He is good and kind. (see Psalm 34:8)
- He is our rock. (see Psalm 62:6)
- He is our hope. (see Psalm 71:5)
- He is all-powerful. (see Luke 1:37)
- He is all-knowing. (see Romans 11:33)
- He is approachable. (see James 4:8)
- He is love. (see 1 John 4:16)

You won't find more impressive "father credentials" than his. God desires to have a close, intimate relationship with you—a father-child relationship. You are never without a father because God is available to you if you reach out to him.

Finding Family Love

Just as you have a spiritual parent available to you, you also have a source for a spiritual family. It comes complete with intergenerational members, although you might all be classified as brothers and sisters. We are referring to the church—that "family" of believers in Jesus Christ. When you accept Christ as your Savior, you automatically gain not only a secure relationship with your heavenly Father, but also join in the membership with "brothers and sisters" in Christ. Your church family can provide the physical companionship of others to build up your life and give you the encouragement you need and desire.

Finding a Role Model

Maybe you have worried that starting your own successful family will be difficult because you didn't have positive role models growing up. Well, you are wise to realize the importance of a good role model, but don't think that none are available to you. That is where the church comes in again. God designed the church for just such a purpose.

The apostle Paul was one of the first itinerant missionaries, and he started churches in various parts of Europe and the Middle East. Christianity (or "The Way" as the early church was called) was brand-new. Paul gave the church specific operating instructions, as well as guidelines on how its members should relate with one another. In particular, he instructed that the older men should be role models for the younger men; and he challenged the older women to pass their wisdom about family life to the younger women (see Titus 2).

While you may have a limited number of positive role models who are related to you genetically, you might be able to find many appropriate role models at your church. Get to know the people there, and look for the families that have the qualities that you want in yours. Then ask them for their wisdom. They will be glad to help you (in part because they'll be flattered that you asked them).

The Ultimate Family Manual

If you were raised in a difficult family situation, or if you're living in one now, you have another resource that includes all the answers that you need for your situation. It is an ancient manual of Middle-Eastern wisdom, a compendium of time-tested and guaranteed wisdom for family life. You may already have a copy of this invaluable treatise: the Bible.

In the pages of this great Book you will learn about how God deals with his children. Those illustrations will tell you much about unconditional love (God's) and disobedience (ours). You'll have a better understanding of both ideal parental love and discipline, and of childish immaturity and rebellion, when you read the Bible.

There Is No Place Like Home

To illustrate God's love for his rebellious children, Jesus told the parable of "the Prodigal Son." This is the story of a wealthy father with two sons. The younger son was greedy, so he said to his father: "I want my share of your estate now because I don't want to wait until you die." (OK, so he was greedy *and* rude.) The father conceded to his request and divided his wealth between his sons.

Before long, the younger son had wasted all of his inheritance in wild partying in a foreign country. At the point of starving, he took a job feeding slop to a farmer's pigs. This job was a mixed blessing. He could eat all he wanted, but he was eating pig slop. The humiliation brought him to his senses. He decided to return home to ask his father's forgiveness and to see if his father would consent to hire him as a servant (so he could end his career as a slop slinger).

The father saw his approaching son, who was a long way down the road. Filled with love and compassion, the father ran to meet him. The father was anxious to be reunited with his son. The young man apologized, and the father declared that a fat calf be killed and barbecued for a celebration banquet.

Of course, there was one person who, like the fatted calf, wasn't happy to see the younger son return. The older brother was jealous that his father had accepted the younger brother back into the family.

The parable of the Prodigal Son is rich with insights about God as our father. It also tells us a lot about ourselves, and how we respond to God as his children. These principles apply to the spiritual relationships between God and humans, but they are also helpful in understanding the dynamics of human families.

In the story of the Prodigal Son, we learn about:

- *Rebellion:* At first we are shocked at the son's greed and disrespect for his father. It is easy to spot in someone else. But his story may make it easier for us to see similar traits in our own lives. We rebel against God when we want to go our own way and do our own thing.

- *Repentance:* The Prodigal Son had to reach the lowest point in his life—a breaking point—before he came to his senses. Sometimes it takes severe events to get us thinking correctly. The son was truly repentant. He didn't make excuses. He accepted the responsibility for his own failings. He was intent on asking for forgiveness from his father. Notice that he didn't ask to be restored to the position of a son (because he didn't feel that he deserved that privilege); he was hoping that he could be a servant. In our relationships with God and with our family members, our repentance should be marked with similar qualities.

There are also some deep lessons that can be learned about God and parenthood by examining the actions and attitudes of the father. Here are two of them:

- *Release:* This father knew his younger son well enough to know that no convincing was going to keep him home. This was a rebellious son who needed to be released. Although it was not the father's preferred choice for his son, there was apparently no other way. The son was going to have to learn the hard way. God must feel the same way about us sometimes when we are so rebellious. He lets us reap the consequences of our own poor choices. And we may need to do the same occasionally with members of our family when no further reasonable efforts will change their behavior.

- *Reconciliation:* The father's response to his returning son is a perfect example of God's love for us. The whole time that the son was away in rebellion, the father was hoping for his return. The story suggests that the father was looking down the road each day in the hope that his son would be returning. When he finally saw his son, he ran out to meet him, "filled with love and compassion." (That response is just the opposite of how most of us would respond. We might make the son grovel and beg for forgiveness.) Our God, as depicted by the prodigal's father, never responds to our sincere requests for forgiveness with an arrogant or self-righteous attitude: reconciliation is always welcomed and immediate. What a lesson for us in terms of dealing with our family members.

But these lessons don't stop there. The older son presents the picture of negative attitudes that shouldn't be part of the reconciliation process:

- *Rejection:* The older son felt rejected. He shouldn't have. His father loved him as much as always. But he was jealous that the younger son was back in the father's good graces. He felt slighted because the younger son had squandered half of the inheritance and the father was still inclined to do nice things for him. This older son had determined that this situation wasn't "fair," but he was viewing it through his own eyes and not from the perspective of his father. He was being self-centered and self-righteous.

- *Resentment:* The older son resented both his father and his younger brother. He viewed himself as "the good son" and his brother as the delinquent. He failed to understand what might be one of the most important lessons of this entire parable. It is obvious to everyone that the younger son rebelled against his father when he lived in the foreign country. But the older son was just as rebellious because he didn't share his father's attitude of love and forgiveness. We can be living in open rebellion toward God (or our family members) in a "foreign" country. But we can also be living in disguised rebellion against God (or our family) in his "house." If we don't share the same attitude of God's heart—if we aren't in sync with him—then we are in rebellion.

The Bible is the story of a family: It is the story of God, the Father, and how he loves and cares for his children who are often rebellious, disrespectful, and immature.

As we understand more about God, we learn about the kind of love he wants us to show to the other members of our family. As we understand more about ourselves, we become a little more forgiving of the failings of our family members because we recognize that we appear the same way to God.

Begin a Legacy of Success

Whether you came from a failing family or whether you are stuck in one now, you can change the circumstances for yourself and the others by exhibiting the traits that make a family successful. The change may not be instantaneous, but you will feel better about your situation because you will be feeling more positive about yourself.

There are many helpful resources available that explain principles and techniques for establishing a successful family that is centered on godly principles. We have listed some of our favorites in the bibliography. But for now, let us give you just three steps that you can work on right away.

Step #1. Get Involved in Your Family

It sounds obvious, but the daily routine of life often makes us strangers even though we live under the same roof. Your "family" may include a spouse and several children. Or, your current situation may define your "family" as parents and siblings who live nearby or in another state. The methods for being involved with your family will be different based on your particular circumstances, but the essence is the same regardless of the time and space continuum in which your family operates.

- *Be Present.* You have to be in contact with each other on a regular basis. There must be opportunities for you to connect with each other. If you share the same house, then this is easier to do (mealtime or the end of the day). If you are living in a different city, then connect via the phone or e-mail. Stay in touch with your family.

- *Be Approachable.* You know from personal experience that there are family members who are present in your life but are not receptive to a meaningful conversation. Don't let your family have that opinion of you. Show interest and concern for what is happening in their lives. Ask questions (and stick around for the answers).

- *Be Understanding.* Recognize that you might be the only one interested in repairing the broken relationships in your family (or at least you may be the only one willing to work at it). Don't be frustrated or impatient if your family members make slow progress in responding to your efforts. When you are tempted to be judgmental or angry at the self-centeredness of your family members, just remember how patient God has been with you.

Step #2. Instill Values in Your Family
This may have been missing in your family for a few generations. It is not too late to start. This is a principle for successful families that God has suggested for centuries. Moses told the Israelites to instill the proper values in their families:

> *Hear, O Israel! The Lord is our God, the Lord alone. And you must love the Lord your God with all your heart, all your soul, and all your strength. And you must commit yourselves wholeheartedly to these commands I am giving you today. Repeat them again and again to your children. Talk about them when you are at home and when you are away on a journey, when you are lying down and when you are getting up again.*
>
> DEUTERONOMY 6: 4-7

Instilling values in your family requires talking about them. It also involves teaching them through your own conduct. A changed behavior on your part in your family relationships may be the greatest lesson about values that your family members ever learn.

Step #3. Show Unconditional Love
The single most effective component in establishing an effective, successful family is unconditional love. This gets us back to the tribute that George W. Bush gave his parents. But a much better example of unconditional love is God himself.

- *There is nothing you can do to make him love you more.* His love for us is not something we have to earn. He doesn't dispense love toward us like bonus points in a video game when we perform well. We have all of his love now. This takes the pressure off of us from being perfect all of the time (which we aren't). His is an unselfish love that extends toward us even though we are unworthy of it.

- *There is nothing you can do to make God love you less.* God doesn't withdraw love when we disappoint him. We don't jeopardize the loss of his love when we screw up. Like the father of the Prodigal Son who was waiting for his son's return, God's love is constant and not reduced when we fail. Such unconditional love makes it easy to return to him from our rebellion because we know that he is anxious to forgive us.

Think about God's unconditional love for you. Let that be your guideline for bringing success into your family.

From Family to Friends

You are born into your family, but you can choose your friends. Failures in your family may not be your fault because you weren't a part of the problem. It might not be so easy to sidestep failure issues when they crop up in relationships with your friends.

It is time to ease you from the family room into the world of other relationships. This is where the going may get a little tougher, but you'll see that failures in this area can be the basis for very successful friendships.

*There is only one influence that converts,
and that is the example of a life which is shot
through and through with the glory
and strength of the spirit of Christ.*

—Hugh Richard and Laurie Sheppard

CHAPTER 4

When Relationships Fail

I n the time it takes you to read this sentence, there will be ten more people living on planet Earth. In the time it takes you to read this paragraph (assuming you aren't a speed reader) there will be one more person living in the United States (although we're not exactly sure where that person is).

We're not trying to scare you into being one of those zero-population advocates. We happen to believe there's plenty of room to spread your wings. Of course, we can't speak for places like Hong Kong or Tokyo, where people are stacked up like cordwood, but we do have some experience with the good old US of A. Recently we crisscrossed the country by car in search of the meaning of life (you can read all about it in our book, *Bruce & Stan Search for the Meaning of Life*), and we found lots of places with all kinds of space.

For example, we drove through Wyoming, where there are fewer than five people per square mile, which is about the same population density as

Outer Mongolia. (In fact, the entire United States has only 75 people per square mile on the average, so you don't have to worry about overcrowding anytime soon.)

What *is* important to think about are the people you relate to in your own few square miles of influence:

- The people in your family
- Your friends, neighbors, and acquaintances
- The people in your school
- Your coworkers
- The people you love ... and the people you don't
- Difficult people and strangers

When you think about it, you talk to, connect with, glance at, pass by, and ignore literally hundreds of people each and every day. Some of these people are the same every day. Others you meet or see only once. The point is that you can't go through your day without relating to people in some way.

And while you're in the process of relating, you might as well admit something to yourself. *Not all relationships are created equal.* Some of your relationships are going to be very positive, some of them are going to be rather ordinary, and some of your relationships are going to stink.

And here's something else to admit. *The quality of your relationships with people is going to change.* In other words, just because you've got a great relationship with someone today doesn't mean it might not turn stinky sometime in the future. On the other hand, a very ordinary relationship with someone you barely know can become exceptional over a period of time.

Your relationships are dynamic, in a constant state of flux, mainly because every person on Earth is dynamic and in a constant state of flux. We are always changing, adapting, adjusting, and compromising our personalities in order to fit the occasion or the situation. If there's one thing we know about people, it's that they are predictable only when they are doing what you expect, which isn't all that often.

The Reality of Failed Relationships

It would be so much fun if we could spend the rest of this chapter talking about those wonderful relationships we all love and cherish. You know the ones. We all have a couple. But that's not what this book is about. We're not here to discuss success; we're here to talk about failure. (OK, so maybe we do talk about success, but not until we wade through the muck and mire of failure first.)

Truth is, every one of us is familiar with failed relationships. We all have plenty in our past, and there will be some in our future. Most painfully, we must admit that we are probably experiencing at least one failed relationship—or at least one that's on the slippery slope to failure—right now. This isn't pessimism. It's reality. It's the inevitable result of imperfect people living together in an imperfect world, working through unpredictable circumstances.

We're not relationship experts in the formal sense, but we have had plenty of experience (so have you). We have read a bunch of books by people who do know what to do when relationships fail (so can you). However, no advice or book—not even this one, believe it or not—can help you to deal successfully with a failed relationship unless you have the desire to first deal with yourself.

This isn't psychological mumbo jumbo. It's the truth. When a relationship starts to go bad, it isn't by accident. There is a sequence of events that happen to you, followed by a series of responses that come from you. You can't necessarily control the things that happen to you, but you can decide how you are going to respond. The problem is that few of us have the awareness or the discipline to interrupt the sequence and prevent the relationship from going south. Here's what we mean.

Picture yourself in a relationship. This could be a hypothetical relationship, or you may want to think of an actual situation you're going through right now. Here is a list of one-on-one relationships to choose from:

- Friend/friend
- Sibling/sibling
- Parent/child
- Student/teacher
- Employee/boss
- Husband/wife

Got a mental picture? OK, let's say that something happens (or a series of things occur in rapid succession) that takes you by *surprise*. The other person in the relationship does something you don't expect, or perhaps that person doesn't do something you think he or she should. Maybe it isn't something that person does so much as something he or she says to offend you.

Your surprise turns to *disappointment* because you expect something better (or at least different), but you don't say anything. You take the "high road" by thinking, "Boy, I would never do that." You immediately begin to mentally formulate a plan of action for the person who has disappointed you. Keep in mind that your plan doesn't involve your own activity, but a course of action you think the other person—we'll call this person the "offender"—should take.

When the offender doesn't respond the way you think he or she should, your disappointment turns to *discouragement*. You begin to wonder if that person is ever going to change or, more specifically, make things right with you. In your mind—again, you haven't shared your thinking with the offender—you have already decided that the offender must apologize in order to satisfy your high standards.

Now, here's where it starts to get ugly. Your discouragement, if left alone, eventually turns to *blame*. You have already decided that nothing about this situation is your fault. Even if you don't know the offender personally, you are 100 percent confident that you have all the information necessary to pass judgment: It's *his (or her)* fault. If this person would only admit the mistake, you wouldn't be having this problem.

Blame is bad news, but we all play the blame game. It starts when we're toddlers in the sandbox. It's the most effective way we have of protecting our fragile egos, and it's also the dumbest, because of what happens next.

A man can fail many times but he isn't a failure until he begins to blame others.

—Ted Engstrom

If left unchecked, blame inevitably turns to *anger,* because no one responds well to blame. Rather than dousing a difficult situation with the cool waters of understanding, blame throws gasoline onto the fire. To get a mental image of blame in action, imagine a baseball game in which the manager is arguing vehemently with an umpire. Each guy is pointing a finger of blame, which further agitates the other person. It's ridiculous, and it never leads to one guy finally saying, "Hey, you know what, you're right. Please accept my apologies. I was wrong." No, blaming always leads to an impasse or to a situation where one person (in this case the person in authority) throws the other person out of the game.

When Anger Goes Bad

Anger in itself isn't necessarily a bad thing. For example, anger can be a great motivator if you are angry at injustice or evil in the world. But anger can go bad, and it usually does, because we don't know how to properly direct it. In his book, *Dare to Discipline Yourself,* Dale Galloway says we mishandle our anger in two ways:

1. We take our anger out on someone else, often someone very close to us.
2. We suppress our anger until one day it explodes, causing great harm.

Anger is a normal emotion, but it is often the cause of failed relationships. We need to learn to control it or express it in healthy ways.

There's one more stage in the events of your hypothetical relationship. If you get to the point of anger and your anger is not dealt with in a healthy manner, the only thing left is *bitterness,* and this may be the most destructive element of all. You think that by being bitter, you will cause the other person to suffer, but in reality, you are the one who will do all the suffering. Bitter people are among the unhappiest people on earth, because they are being eaten from the inside out by a variety of emotions, none of them good.

The Handbook of Bible Application states: "Like a small root that grows into a great tree, bitterness springs up in our heart and overshadows even our deepest Christian relationships. A 'bitter root' comes when we allow disappointment to grow into resentment, or when we nurse grudges over past hurts."

There you have it. A little something we like to call the *Six Stages of Relationship Failure*. Let's review them (feel free to squirm):

- Stage 1: *Surprise*
- Stage 2: *Disappointment*
- Stage 3: *Discouragement*
- Stage 4: *Blame*
- Stage 5: *Anger*
- Stage 6: *Bitterness*

So What Do We Do About It?

These are the things that happen all too often in our relationships, but it doesn't have to be that way. The *Six Stages of Relationship Failure* aren't inevitable. You don't have to get on this slippery slope, and if you are already on it, you can jump off at any time. No one is forcing you to slide from surprise to bitterness. *The choice is yours.*

The Bible says something very important about this process. Read this carefully:

> *Get rid of all bitterness, rage, anger, harsh words, and slander, as well as all types of malicious behavior. Instead, be kind to each other, tenderhearted, forgiving one another, just as God through Christ has forgiven you.*
> EPHESIANS 4:31-32

The only person who can take responsibility for a failed or a failing relationship is *you*. As much as you believe it's the other person's fault, you can't control what the other person does or how the other person feels. The only person you can control is you. The Bible doesn't say, "Ask the other person to get rid of all ..." You are the one who must take action. The question is *how*. (Gee, we thought you'd never ask).

Since you're asking, it's only right and proper that we answer you the best we can. With a lot of help from the Bible and some very wise contemporary writers, we have assembled *Ten Ways to Build Healthy Relationships*. This isn't a "pick and choose" list. Each of these elements is like a building block. If you leave one of them out of your life, things aren't going to necessarily fall apart, but your life won't be complete, and you will always be susceptible to failed relationships.

Here's something else to keep in mind. None of us can do these things on our own. We need the help and power of the Holy Spirit. Our natural, sinful natures will produce disappointment, anger, and bitterness. But the Holy Spirit will produce the kind of life that leads to healthy relationships if you give control of your life over to him (read Galatians 5:16-26). Here's what the apostle Paul recommends:

> *So I advise you to live according to your new life in the Holy Spirit. Then you won't be doing what your sinful nature craves. The old sinful nature loves to do evil, which is the opposite from what the Holy Spirit wants. And the Spirit gives us desires that are opposite from what the sinful nature desires. These two forces are constantly fighting each other, and your choices are never free from this conflict.*

GALATIANS 5:16-18

Ten Ways to Build Healthy Relationships

In each of these ten ways for building healthy relationships, we will give you the spiritual *principle* (this is what happens when the Holy Spirit controls your life) and the opposing human *tendency* (this is what happens when sin controls your life). Remember, these things don't happen to you automatically. It's always a choice.

Choice #1. Love Others or Love Yourself

Like a bad actor in a movie, love has become miscast in our culture. People talk about love, but few know how to express it the way God intended. Oh, we're good at expressing *affection* for everything from our pets to our possessions, but that comes and goes according to our moods. *Friendship* is another kind of love we love to engage, but true friendships are hard to come by and easy to break. Then there's *sex*, which is a type of love (the

Greeks called it *eros*, the root of the word *erotic*), but with the greatest capacity of all to abuse true love.

Now, affection and friendship are fine as long as another aspect of love is present (and sex is great as long as you're married). However, what is still needed is the only love that is completely other-centered: *agape* love. This is what the great writer C.S. Lewis called "Divine Gift-Love," because when we love with *agape* love we desire the best for the people we love. Here's how the Bible defines *agape* love:

Love is patient and kind. Love is not jealous or boastful or proud or rude. Love does not demand its own way. Love is not irritable, and it keeps no record of when it has been wronged. It is never glad about injustice but rejoices whenever the truth wins out. Love never gives up, never loses faith, is always hopeful, and endures through every circumstance.

1 CORINTHIANS 13:4-7

The only way we can have this kind of love is to give control of our lives over to the Holy Spirit. We need to recognize that God is the example and source of other-centered, self-sacrificing love. The reason we are capable of loving others in this manner is because God loved us this way first (see 1 John 4: 9-10). Love is the first building block of healthy relationships. When you truly love others, you are saying, "I want the best for you."

Choice #2. Serve Others or Use Others
The slogan at the Hard Rock Café in Atlanta is a good one: *Love y'all, serve y'all.* We like that because it clearly shows that serving others is the natural result of loving others. God showed his love for us when he sent Jesus Christ into the world to take away our sins (see 1 John 4:9-10). And even though Jesus was God, he willingly gave up his rights and took on the position of a servant (see Philippians 2:5-7). Jesus made the ultimate sacrifice by giving up his own life for ours.

You may never have to give your life for someone, but you can never escape the responsibility of serving others, no matter who they are. Here's what Jesus said:

You know that in this world kings are tyrants, and officials lord it over the people beneath them. But among you it should be quite different. Whoever wants to be a leader among you must be your servant, and whoever wants to be first must become your slave. For even I, the Son of Man, came here not to be served but to serve others, and to give my live as a ransom for many.

MATTHEW 20:25-28

Service is the second building block of healthy relationships. When you truly serve others, you are saying, "What can I do for you?"

Choice #3: Trust Others or Distrust Others

People can be so cynical. We think everyone (especially auto mechanics and IRS agents) are out to take advantage of us, so we take the easy road and simply refuse to trust anyone until they prove themselves trustworthy. Even when it comes to our own friends and family, we become cynical. Rather than seeing the best in people, we look for hidden motives, much as a detective searches for clues. OK, so you may uncover some incriminating evidence, but is that really the way you want to live your life? Even the law of the land says, "Innocent until proven guilty."

Just like the principles of love and service, we must look to God first when it comes to trust, and that isn't always easy. First of all, it's hard to trust God if you don't know him. If you simply rely on the opinions of others, you might come to distrust God as much as the next cynic. But if you search the Bible and uncover the truth about God, you will find that he is completely trustworthy and true.

Trust in the Lord with all your heart; do not depend on your own understanding. Seek his will in all you do, and he will direct your paths.

PROVERBS 3:5-6

As you trust God, he will show himself to be faithful in the circumstances of your life. The same thing goes for other people. As you trust them with love and patience, they will respond to you. Sometimes people betray our confidence because we don't trust them in the first place. Trust is the third building block of healthy relationships. When you trust others, you are saying, "I respect you."

Choice #4: Listen to Others or Argue With Others

Both of us are intrigued by political talk shows. You know the ones, where a host (usually an irascible person) confronts a guest with pointed questions and accusations. Or sometimes two people with opposite ideologies square off in a heated debate about the issue of the week. What all these shows have in common is that nobody listens to anybody else. Rather than hearing out the points the other person is making, each side literally talks over the other person until all you have is a shouting match. It's ridiculous, but it's also illustrative of how people relate to one another.

Now, you may not have the audacity to talk over someone else when they're talking to you, but you don't have to. You can simply stare at the other person while they're going on and on about some topic as your brain formulates responses, or simply thinks about something else entirely. When this happens, you aren't hearing actual words, but something more like *blah, blah, blah.*

Truly listening to another person is one of the greatest gifts you can give. By contrast, failing to listen to others is one of the greatest contributors to failed relationships. Spouses do it to each other, parents do it to children, friends do it to friends, and it buries communication. If left unchecked, failing to listen will eventually kill a relationship.

Once again, we need to go to God for our example on how to listen. Did you know that God not only hears but listens to us 100 percent of the time? The psalmist David wrote: "The Lord has heard my plea; the Lord will answer my prayer" (Psalm 6:9). At the same time, the Bible tells us to "listen carefully" to everything God has told us through his Word (Deuteronomy 5:1). As we learn to listen to God, we will learn to listen to others. In the process, we will learn that listening will keep us from doing something we might later regret:

My dear brothers and sisters, be quick to listen, slow to speak, and slow to get angry. Your anger can never make things right in God's sight.

JAMES 1:19-20

How to Listen

Listening isn't something that comes naturally for us. It takes study, effort, and practice. In his book, *Becoming a Person of Influence*, Dr. John Maxwell suggests these nine ways to improve your listening skills:

1. Look at the speaker.
2. Don't interrupt.
3. Focus on understanding.
4. Determine the need of the moment.
5. Check your emotions.
6. Suspend your judgment.
7. Sum up at major intervals.
8. Ask questions for clarity.
9. Always make listening your priority.

Listening is the fourth building block of healthy relationships. When you listen to others, you are saying, "I hear you."

Choice #5: Encourage Others or Discourage Others

In his excellent book, *The Friendship Factor*, Dr. Alan McGinnis writes: "If you are looking for a way to increase your success with people, master the art of affirmation."

McGinnis quotes Dale Carnegie, who wrote *How to Win Friends and Influence People* (another great book on building healthy relationships). Carnegie's "Big Secret of Dealing With People" is this: "Be hearty in your approbation and lavish in your praise." Now, we've got to be honest and tell you that we had to look up "approbation." Here's the definition we found: "To express approval or show appreciation."

Isn't that the essence of encouragement? Why are we so stingy with our words of encouragement? We think it has to do with our own lack of confidence. We're afraid that if we encourage someone else too much, it might detract from us. But isn't that the point? Remember the principle of *agape* love? When you truly love someone, you *want* the best for him or her.

Similarly, when you encourage someone, you *see* the best in him or her. We're not talking about false praise (of the kiss-up variety). This is the kind of praise that builds others up rather than tearing them down.

> *So encourage each other and build each other up, just as you are already doing.*
> 1 THESSALONIANS 5:11

Encouragement is the fifth building block of healthy relationships. When you encourage others, you are saying, "I admire you."

Choice #6: Learn From Others or Ignore Others

There's only one way to gain knowledge, and that's to learn. And there's only one way to learn, and that's to learn from others.

Now, there are different ways to learn from others. You can learn by reading books others have written ("Reading is to the mind what exercise is to the body," wrote Richard Steele). You can also learn by watching television and interacting with other media (although we don't recommend it as much as reading ... in most cases, you have to wade through a lot of junk before you get to the stuff that will help you).

And you can also learn from other people. The good thing about learning from others is that it helps to build relationships. When you tell someone that you want to learn from him or her, you show that person tremendous respect. And it's not just a one-way street. One of the most valuable relationships you can have is to be a student to a teacher or mentor. It's a powerful connection that enlarges your world even as it empowers you to be more than you are.

Learning from others is the sixth building block of healthy relationships. When you learn from others, you are saying, "I am a better person because you are teaching me."

Choice #7: Teach Others or Deny Others

Not everyone is cut out to be a teacher, but all of us should teach. We're not talking about imparting your wondrous knowledge in a way that's arrogant and trivial and drives other people away (like Cliff the mailman used to do on *Cheers*). We mean the kind of teaching that has to do with helping others become better people.

It's important to share the gifts God gives to us with other people. Maybe you're good at electronics or computers. There's someone out there who would love to know what you know. Perhaps you know a little something about finances and investments. A lot of people aren't too good in this area. By teaching others who would love to learn even a fraction of what you know, you would be doing them a great service.

The thing is, teaching takes time. It means sacrificing and giving of yourself in a way that might not be convenient. But that's what healthy relationships are all about—one person giving to another in ways that aren't always convenient. Probably the best example of where this needs to happen is between a parent and a child. If you are a parent, you know what we mean. If you aren't, pay attention anyway. This is good stuff, because it's right from the Bible. As a parent, you are responsible to teach your children about God and his principles for living.

Repeat them again and again to your children. Talk about them when you are at home and when you are away on a journey, when you are lying down and when you are getting up again.
                                                                    DEUTERONOMY 6:7

Teaching others is a gift we all must give. It's also the seventh building block of healthy relationships. When you teach others, you are saying, "There's something important I want to tell you."

Choice #8: Forgive Others or Hold a Grudge
Oh boy, this is a big one. If you desire to stop the trend of failed relationships in your life, you need to learn the act of forgiveness. "Forgiveness is a choice," write John Nieder and Thomas Thompson in their book, *Forgive and Love Again.* "God won't make you forgive those who hurt you."

Hurt is a big issue in life. We've all been wronged by others, and sometimes the pain that comes from the hurt seems unbearable. We want so much for the person who hurts us to come and say, "I'm sorry for what I did." But that doesn't always happen. It's pointless and unproductive for us to wait for someone else to apologize. We must take the first step by offering forgiveness.

By failing to forgive, we hurt only ourselves. Nieder and Thompson give four consequences to unforgiveness:

- Unforgiveness imprisons you in your past because it keeps the pain alive.
- Unforgiveness breeds bitterness and resentment and anger.
- Unforgiveness and anger give Satan "a mighty foothold" (Ephesians 4:27).
- Unforgiveness hinders your fellowship with God (see Matthew 6:14-15).

By contrast, when you forgive, you are being obedient to God and you are recognizing that God has already forgiven you (see Ephesians 4:31-32). Forgiveness is the eighth building block of healthy relationships. When you forgive others, you are saying, "I love you too much to carry a grudge."

Forgiveness is a door to peace and happiness.
It is a small, narrow door, and cannot
be entered without stooping.

—Johann Christoph Arnold

Choice #9: Ask for Forgiveness or Let Pride Get in the Way

Getting forgiveness is just as important as giving it to others. Have you done something recently that hurt someone else? Or it may be for something that happened a while ago. In his autobiography, *The Wounded Spirit*, Frank Peretti describes the way he was mercilessly teased and bullied as a youngster. "I know how the abuse in my youth hurt me deeply and still affects me today," he writes. But Peretti doesn't dwell on his own hurts. Instead, he turns the tables and thinks about the teasing he dished out, and he asks us to do the same. "How many people are still wounded because of what you or I did to them?" he asks us.

The first thing to do is to "wake up to what you've done and what you may still be doing," says Peretti. "Are you inflicting wounds on others?"

Second, we need to ask God for forgiveness. If we confess our sins to God, he has promised to forgive us (see 1 John 1:9).

Third, we need to ask God to change our hearts and make us more like Jesus, who never took "cruel advantage of anyone's disadvantage."

Fourth, we need to serve others whenever and wherever we can. "Rather than flaunting our gifts, our success, our popularity, our privilege, we should realize that it's time to be noble and consider those gifts for what they are: our means, our resources by which we are to help others."

Finally, if possible, we need to go to those we have wronged and hurt and ask forgiveness. It's never too late. Asking forgiveness is the ninth building block in healthy relationships. When we ask forgiveness of others, we are saying, "I have wronged you."

Choice #10: Pray for Others or Think Only of Yourself

Are you getting the idea that failed relationships happen because we focus on ourselves rather than others? In every one of these ten ways to build healthy relationships, it's vital to focus on other people. One of the greatest ways to do this is through prayer.

In our book *Bruce & Stan's Pocket Guide to Talking With God,* we make the point that prayer is the way we communicate with God. Prayer is God's gift to us because it gives us access to "the throne of our gracious God" (Hebrews 4:12). You don't need an appointment, and you don't need any special skills. God is willing and anxious to listen to your prayers anytime you have the urge to talk with him (which should be often).

If prayer is God's gift to us, then our prayer for others is our gift to them. The apostle Paul wrote to the church in Colossae: "We always pray for you" (Colossians 1:3). Don't just pray for "all the missionaries in China." Be specific. Read Colossians 1:3-14 and see how specific Paul was in his prayer for others. He prayed for their needs, he prayed for their relationship with God, and he prayed that they would have endurance, patience, and joy. Your prayers are powerful, especially when you pray on behalf of others.

The earnest prayer of a righteous person has great power and wonderful results.

JAMES 5:16

Praying for others is the tenth building block of a healthy relationship. When we pray for others, we are saying, "I want God's best for you."

Helping Others Succeed

If you take away only one thing from this chapter, it should be this: *The way to keep your relationships from failing is to help others succeed.* The reason people have trouble developing and keeping meaningful relationships is that they keep the focus on themselves. But it doesn't have to be that way. The moment you change your attitude from "What can you do for me?" to "What can I do for you?" you will succeed in your relationships.

Something else will happen when you make this critical adjustment in your thinking. You will become a person of influence. How do we know? Because influential people get that way by putting the needs of others before their own. Not only that, but they understand what John Maxwell calls the "levels of influence."

Level One: Modeling

This has nothing to do with appearing in the Sears catalog. Modeling means you become an example to many people, even those you don't know personally. When your life takes on the ten characteristics from the preceding section, people notice you.

Our lives are a fragrance presented by Christ to God.

2 CORINTHIANS 2:15

Level Two: Motivating

This doesn't mean you get on the motivational speaking circuit like Matt Foley. A motivator is one who encourages and relates to people on a heart-to-heart level.

So encourage each other and build each other up.

1 THESSALONIANS 5:11

Level Three: Mentoring

The essence of mentoring is helping others reach their potential. You need at least one mentor in your life, but you also need to mentor others. The apostle Paul was the consummate mentor. Timothy was his "true in the faith" even though they were peers. Mentoring isn't just a guy thing, either. Paul wrote:

These older women must train the younger women.

TITUS 2:4

As for the men:

In the same way, encourage the young men to live wisely in all they do.

TITUS 2:6

Level Four: Multiplying

This is the ultimate level of influence. This is where you help the people you are influencing to become influencers of others. Jesus was the ultimate model, motivator, mentor, and multiplier. He lived his life as the perfect model for all people; he motivated others to seek God; he mentored his disciples; and he taught them to go out and do the same. Now, two thousand years later, his influence is felt by billions of people.

More Than Influence

Becoming a person of influence is a worthwhile goal to have throughout your life. Others will be drawn to you and your relationships will improve as you do your best to help others succeed. But there is a certain kind of relationship that requires more than mere influence. This relationship asks more than simply helping the other person succeed.

We're referring to the kind of love that leads to and comes from marriage. Call it romance, call it love for a lifetime, or call it the ultimate love between a man and a woman. Whatever it is to you, this love is unique, and it requires a unique approach.

The next chapter is all about this extraordinary kind of love, the kind that can lead to great joy or equally great feelings of failure. Whether you are happily married or happily single—or just the opposite—we encourage you to read it with an open mind and an open heart.

> Love is what makes the world go around—
> that and clichés.

—Michael Brooke Symons

CHAPTER 5

When You Lose at Love

This chapter may hurt the most. Failure in every other area of life will get you some sympathy, but striking out at romance will make you the object of effusive pity. No one will laugh at you if you are reading the "help wanted" ads when you come up short in your career, but you could be subject to the ultimate indignity and humiliation if you are discovered reading the personal ads.

The social stigma that is attached to failures of the romantic variety is not an unexplored phenomenon. Research studies and surveys have analyzed the pressure people feel to be "paired up." But on something this obvious, we prefer to be guided in our analysis by our own gastrointestinal promptings. In other words, we go with our gut reaction. And it is our gut reaction that people are hypersensitive to feelings of failure in romance because:

> **"Couples" are viewed as the norm.**
> **Individuals are simply one-half of a couple.**
> **If you don't have a corresponding half,**
> **then you are incomplete.**

The Noah Mentality

We call it the "Noah" mentality. It is a belief that life works best when it is lived two-by-two. This fixation with "couples" has been insidiously instilled into our culture by a variety of sources:

- *Restaurants:* Did you ever notice that seating in restaurants is predominantly geared for couples? The tables are set for patrons in multiples of two. When was the last time you saw a restaurant table set for three? And you never see a table set for just one. They just seat you at a table set for two, then make an elaborate show of removing the extra set.

- *Automobile Manufacturers:* Seating in cars always starts out with two. Even as car companies are searching for the most fuel-efficient design for so-called commuter cars, they put in two seats. Whether it is an economy, sport, or luxury vehicle, the front seat is designed for a couple. Even the second seat is often designed for two (the "spare" person has to ride with his knees under his chin). The only exceptions are the "family vans" that can accommodate an odd number of children (but doesn't the mere prospect of child passengers presume that you are part of a couple that procreated those progeny?).

- *Religion:* Some people mistakenly believe that the Bible mandates marriage. They are quick to quote from Genesis 1:28, where God said to Adam and Eve: "Be fruitful, and multiply, and populate the earth." (At least that's how God might have sounded if he had spoken in the old King James English.) Well, we've got news for those who use this verse as a divine direction that everyone should marry: The world has now been populated. It's OK to stop! (Even the apostle Paul indicated that not everyone is supposed to be married, but he wasn't basing his opinion on the overpopulation problem.)

- *Television and Movies:* The entertainment industry is fixated on couples. Whether the plotline involves a large group (like the cast from the sitcom "Friends") or a single individual (as in the movie *Castaway*), the story line involves one or more finding the love of their lives.

There is a little bit more to the Noah mentality than simply quantity (which would be "t-w-o" for those of you who need it spelled out again). The Noah mentality also involves quality: the two people must be in love with each other. That doesn't happen automatically with every two people. There are lots of situations where two people are paired together but they aren't in love. (A professional wrestling match is an example.)

Those animals that walked up the ramp to the ark must have been compatible (at least for forty days and forty nights, plus the year it took for the mud to dry). The Noah mentality presupposes the ideal situation of a man and a woman who are in love and at all times perfectly compatible with each other as the definition of success; anything less constitutes failure.

Quantity and Quality

In a culture that has been inculcated with this Noah mentality, it is understandable that you might be feeling like a failure if the "couple thing" hasn't clicked yet in your life. If you have adopted the Noah mentality into your personal belief system, then your cranium may be convulsing with cognitive dissonance for one of two reasons:

- **You feel like a failure because you lack the requisite** *quantity.* There is just one of you. You haven't yet found the love of your life (although you may have done more exploring than Magellan). You are worried that there might not be another "half" for you, after all. You feel as though you have failed at romance because you presently have no one to love, and no one who loves you back.

- **You feel like a failure because you lack the requisite *quality*.** Maybe you are part of a permanent couple, but you have this sinking feeling that you married the wrong person. Your spouse won't change (despite your best efforts to coerce compliance from him or her). You never have fun anymore. And you feel like you have failed at marriage because you presently aren't receiving love so you don't feel like giving love.

In this chapter, we will challenge some of the misconceptions of the Noah mentality. For those of you who feel like you are lacking the requisite quantity, we will present a few perspectives that may help you realize that "1" may be a more successful number than "2," at least for now. If you feel you are lacking the requisite quality, we will discuss several alternative approaches that may change your failing relationship into a successful marriage.

One Is a Whole Number

No other individual is necessary to make you a whole person. Of course, you already knew that, although our words might sound hollow if you aren't feeling whole. But that void could be due to something other than your missing "soul mate." Maybe what you are feeling is just a missing part of you (and we're not referring to body parts removed during your recent appendectomy).

God designed you to be a multidimensional being. We see this most clearly in the life of Christ. The Bible tells a lot about the birth of Jesus (that would be the Christmas story), and it gives a detailed account of his life from the time he was about thirty years old. But most of the life of Jesus during his childhood and early adult life is unreported. There is, however, one very interesting, cryptic verse that covers this time period:

So Jesus grew both in height and in wisdom, and he was loved by God and by all who knew him.

LUKE 2:52

This verse helps identify the four dimensions of Christ's life:

- *Physical:* There was a physical dimension to his life because he grew in height.
- *Mental:* He also grew in wisdom. Just as he grew physically, he also matured intellectually.
- *Spiritual:* He was loved by God, but it wasn't a one-sided relationship. Jesus made his relationship with God a priority.
- *Social:* He was not cloistered away in a monastery. Jesus came into contact with people, and they loved him because of the way he responded to them.

A Look at the "Total You"

Your life won't be operating as God designed it if you are ignoring one or more essential areas. Check the dimensions of your life. (We are not suggesting use of a tape measure, although that may be part of your assessment of the "physical" area.)

Is part of your life out of whack? Do you have unhealthy eating habits? Is your brain getting enough stimulation, or has it been disengaged for a while? Is your spiritual life in a rut (or have you overlooked it entirely)? Do you have solid friendships that are an integral part of your life?

If you are feeling a void in your life, don't assume that your feelings are due to a lack of quantity. Maybe it's simply a matter of getting your life in balance. When all of the dimensions of your life are in balance, you will be surprised at how fulfilling the number "1" can be.

When "1" Still Isn't Enough

Perhaps you have your four dimensions in balance, but you still have a big hole in your life (a hole in the shape that another person would fill nicely). The fact that you have not made the love connection yet doesn't mean that it won't happen at all, and the apparent delay in the process doesn't mean that you are a failure. As difficult as it may be to stay objective, try looking at your circumstances with a positive perspective:

- **Life hasn't passed you by. The timing hasn't been right yet.** Just because you have been waiting doesn't mean that the time was wasted. You have been maturing during that time (hopefully), and the same may be true of the person who will eventually become your spouse. Your personalities and outlook may have been changing. Maybe it was necessary for the time to pass to provide both of you with the opportunity to change enough to become permanently compatible.

- **The fact that you aren't already married doesn't mean there is a problem with you.** Even a broken engagement may be a better indication of your effective screening ability than your ability to sustain a long-term relationship.

Not every successful engagement ends in a marriage. The whole purpose of engagement is for a couple to get to know each other more deeply, to discover any incompatibility. If a couple gets married, it doesn't prove they are compatible. (It may mean only that the engagement period wasn't long enough for the couple to learn everything they needed to know about each other).

You can apply that same logic to dating relationships. The termination of a relationship doesn't mean that you have failed. It means you have successfully identified why that other person is not a prospective spouse for you.

> It is infinitely better to remain single
> than to marry the wrong person.

Wipe That Fear off Your Face

We know what's really bothering you. You wouldn't mind waiting to find the right person just so long as you knew that it was really going to happen. But you don't know for sure, and the longer it goes without happening, the more you worry that it will never occur. As more time passes, that worry turns into all-out fear. But it is more than just the fear that you won't be married. Your imagination makes it worse than that. You begin to fear that you'll live a solitary life as a missionary in the Gobi Desert or as the sole researcher in a lunar space station.

Well, your best bet is to excise the panic from your life. It isn't doing you any good. First of all, it is creating excess stomach acid that sours your breath (and that can't help the prospects for effective dating). Secondly, it changes your behavior. Desperation can make you overanalyze every conversation with anyone who might even remotely be a candidate in your future spousal sweepstakes. You can never relax or be yourself. You can't enjoy the present because you are preoccupied with wondering if each moment has future (e.g., "matrimonial") significance.

A Divine Design

Did it ever occur to you that God knows exactly who is right for you? (That kind of information is available to God. It comes from being omniscient.) And if that is true (which it is), then why isn't God telling you? Doesn't he know that you would be willing to be more patient if you knew the specifics of *if, who,* and *when?*

Maybe there is a purpose to all of this waiting. Maybe God is trying to teach you a few things about yourself ... and himself. Maybe he is trying to teach you patience. (Nah, that's too obvious and downright sadistic on his part.) Maybe he is trying to teach you to depend upon him in your circumstances instead of depending upon yourself (and that Internet dating service). And maybe he wants you to trust his judgment for what is best in your life.

God knows what he is doing, where people are concerned. After all, he designed and manufactured the first prototypes. If it hadn't been for God, Adam and Eve never would have gotten together. According to Genesis 2:

- God knew that Adam needed a companion before Adam became aware of the fact (see Genesis 2:18).

- Eve was custom-designed by God. He handcrafted her (see Genesis 2:21-22).

- She was specifically intended by God to be compatible with Adam (see Genesis 2:20-22).

Except for the fact that you are a little more fashion-conscious than the first human prototypes (we hope), there is not a lot of difference between you and them where mates are concerned. Since God was interested in making sure that Adam and Eve each had suitable spouses, we can trust his judgment—and timing—for ours.

When "Happily Married" Couples ... Aren't

Let's shift from talking about the person who feels like a failure because he or she doesn't have a spouse to the couple who feel like failures because their marriage hasn't turned out as they had hoped.

The quality of a marriage relationship can be measured in many different ways. A study at the Institute for Family Research and Education at Syracuse University identified ten elements as being important in a marriage:

1. *Love.* This seems obvious, but it doesn't exist in all marriages. Each spouse needs to be the recipient of consistent, caring, and sensitive behavior shown in large and small ways. Love needs to be conveyed by words and actions. The lack of displayed love produces hurt feelings and alienation.

2. *Sense of Humor.* Humor brings a sense of balance to daily life. It relieves stress and tension that otherwise develop in daily life and in every marriage. Without laughter, there is a risk that friction will not be dissipated.

3. *Friendships.* Every married couple should have meaningful friendships with other couples. And each spouse should have a few friends. A marriage that is cut off from other significant relationships loses perspective.

4. *Involvement.* Activities outside of the job and the house can provide each spouse with a sense of purpose.

5. *Physical intimacy.* The expression of shared intimacy is an important part of marriage.

6. *Communication.* Conversation is an important part of a healthy marriage. The dialogue carries more than just information. It is a vehicle for expressing feelings.

7. *Sharing.* Marriage is a cooperative arrangement. There needs to be a willingness on the part of both spouses to share in the responsibilities and duties.

8. *Integrity.* Each spouse needs to be dependable and trustworthy.

9. *Adaptability.* Personal growth should be anticipated. Each spouse should appreciate the growth of the other spouse.

10. *Tolerance.* There needs to be an acceptance and forgiveness of the other spouse's mistakes. Although mistakes don't need to be ignored, they should be discussed in a way that is not detrimental to the relationship.

The quality of the marriage can be jeopardized when any aspect of the relationship between the husband and wife is ignored. If both spouses are committed to improving their relationship, then the risk of harm is avoided. But, the case is tragic when only one of the spouses recognizes or is willing to deal with the problem.

You might be feeling like your marriage is a failure if you are trapped in a situation where your spouse is oblivious to a problem or unwilling to make changes that are necessary to remedy an ailing relationship. In such circumstances, you may be tempted to reciprocate with an equally recalcitrant attitude. That would be a natural reaction, and it is understandable. But it is not the action that will improve your circumstances. To turn your failing marriage into a successful one, you may need to do the opposite of what comes naturally.

Dear Abby

The Bible tells the story of a woman, Abigail, who was trapped in a failing marriage. Hers is a story of contraintuitive behavior—doing the opposite of what comes naturally. But her surprising behavior had successful results.

The story of Abigail and her husband, Nabal, is told in 1 Samuel 25. Nabal was a farmer and rancher. His name meant "fool." You might be surprised that any parents would give their child such a name, but in Nabal's case it was well suited.

David (of Goliath fame) was a young man with a small army that protected the local citizens from robbers and invaders. (He was a sort of Robin Hood of his day.) The neighbors subsidized David's army with food and supplies. When David sent his messengers to Nabal for his contribution, Nabal refused. In fact, he even insulted David in the process: "Should I take my bread and water and the meat I've slaughtered for my shearers and give it to a band of outlaws who come from who knows where?" (1 Samuel 25:11).

When David received the message of Nabal's ingratitude, he prepared for battle. He strapped on his sword (by this time he had outgrown the slingshot), and together with four hundred of his men, he rode toward Nabal's ranch with the intention of obliterating everything and everyone in sight.

Meanwhile, back at the ranch, the Nabal's servants had informed Abigail of her husband's stupidity. Without telling her husband, she gathered up enough supplies for David's entire army, and she took a shortcut to intercept David. She interceded on her husband's behalf. She apologized to David for not anticipating the situation. As she gave David all of her supplies, she begged for David's forgiveness and mercy. David accepted her gifts and granted her plea with this statement:

Praise the Lord, the God of Israel, who has sent you to meet me today! Thank God for your good sense! Bless you for keeping me from murdering the man and carrying out vengeance with my own hands. For I swear by the Lord, the God of Israel, who has kept me from hurting you, that if you had not hurried out to meet me, not one of Nabal's men would be alive tomorrow morning.... Return home in peace. We will not kill your husband.

1 SAMUEL 25:32-35

You need to read Abigail's story in its entirety to get the full sense of this woman's situation. She was in a relationship that by all outward standards was a failure. Yet, she rose above the failings of her husband, and compensated for them with her own exemplary behavior. While others might have been tempted to respond with bitterness, Abigail displayed:

- *Attractiveness.* The Bible describes her as a beautiful and sensible woman. She was attractive on both the inside and the outside. Although her husband may have been rude, crude, and disgusting, she maintained her appearance and her attitude.

- *Perceptivity.* She didn't become closed-minded like her husband. She was sensitive to other people's feelings. The servants knew that she was the one who could handle the crisis.

- *Protection.* While Nabal put himself and the rest of his household at great risk, Abigail protected her family by covering for his mistakes. She even protected him from further folly by concealing from him the fact that she was going to attempt reconciliation with David. If Nabal had known of that attempt, he would have blown it for sure.

- *Action.* Abigail did not hesitate to make a personal sacrifice, at great inconvenience and risk to herself, for the sake of her husband.

- *Humility.* Most people can't even apologize for their own mistakes, but Abigail took personal responsibility for her husband's blunder. She was humble and repentant as she pleaded on her husband's behalf.

- *Commitment.* Although he didn't deserve it, Abigail was devoted to her husband. While she had every reason to abandon this buffoon to the consequences of his own folly, she remained loyal to him.

You already know part of the ending of the story: David relented and Nabal was spared. So it proved to be a successful outcome for Nabal, but what of poor Abigail? Well, there was a successful ending for her as well, and here is the rest of the story:

> *When Abigail arrived home, she found that Nabal had thrown a big party and was celebrating like a king. He was very drunk, so she didn't tell him anything about her meeting with David until the next morning. The next morning when he was sober, she told him what had happened. As a result he had a stroke, and he lay on his bed paralyzed. About ten days later, the Lord struck him and he died. When David heard that Nabal was dead ... he wasted no time in sending messengers to Abigail to ask her to become his wife.... And so she became his wife.*
>
> 1 SAMUEL 25:36-42

Don't infer a point that we aren't intending to imply. We aren't saying that God will rescue the innocent spouse from a failing marriage by killing off the arrogant spouse. That's not the point of the story (although it did bring a nice bit of divine justice at the end). We think the lesson from the life of Abigail is the continual display of love toward a spouse that did not reciprocate. In those circumstances, loving behavior was not the natural reaction, but it was the conduct that Abigail chose to exhibit. Her behavior kept a bad situation from getting worse, and it eventually proved to be a successful approach.

Putting Love to the Test

The affirmations of love between a bride and a groom are easily spoken at the wedding altar. They are more difficult to put into practice as time goes on and one spouse becomes self-centered and the other spouse struggles with the temptation to retaliate. But the method for avoiding the complete failure of the marriage is found in the definition of love itself.

If you are in the difficult circumstance of a marriage that is teetering on the brink of failure, remember these words:

Love is patient and kind. Love is not jealous or boastful or proud or rude. Love does not demand its own way. Love is not irritable, and it keeps no record of when it has been wronged. It is never glad about injustice but rejoices whenever the truth wins out. Love never gives up, never loses faith, is always hopeful and endures through every circumstance.

1 CORINTHIANS 13:4-7

The situation in your marriage may not immediately change, but any personal feelings of failure will be replaced with the confident knowledge that you are following God's pattern for success.

What Do You Expect?

Whether you are struggling with the quantity or quality factors, feelings of failure are less likely to envelop you if your expectations are realistic. The whole problem of the Noah mentality arises because people are too idealistic about love and marriage. Instead of comparing your situation to some storybook, idealized, romantic notion, bring your expectations into the realm of reality. This doesn't mean that you should compromise your beliefs and standards, but you must not condemn yourself for failing to obtain something that doesn't exist.

- *Be realistic about love.* There is an ebb and flow to feelings and emotions. They can fluctuate like the stock market. Mature love is more than feelings. It involves a sense of commitment that transcends momentary feelings that can be influenced by mood, lighting, and scented candles.

- *Be realistic about marriage* (present or future). No marriage is without conflict and tension from time to time. Yours won't be any different. Your love and commitment won't erase your humanity.

- *Be realistic about your spouse* (present or future). There is no such thing as an "ideal" spouse. And if you think you have found one, then you are obviously blind to this person's defects. If you are waiting for an "ideal" person to marry, you will disqualify every candidate because no person is without faults. If you are already married, stop comparing your spouse to that "ideal" person who doesn't really exist.

- *Be realistic about yourself.* There is no one person who can meet all of your needs. Remember that there is a spiritual dimension of your life, and no spouse is capable of meeting your needs in that area. Some of what you need can be provided only by God.

> **Your best chance at finding true love is to first find love from the One who is true.**

Love in the Workplace

No, we aren't talking about romance at the office, and we aren't talking about dating your boss. We are assuming that we've discussed your love life enough in the last fourteen pages to last you a while. It's time to get back to work. Speaking of work (how was that for a smooth transition?), do you feel like your career is doomed to failure? As with the other areas of your life, you can take the failures in your occupation and turn them into the foundation of future success. That's what the next chapter is all about.

> It is impossible to get exhausted in work for God.
> We get exhausted because we try to do
> God's work in our own way.

—Oswald Chambers

CHAPTER 6

When Your Career Path
Becomes a Road to Nowhere

No one who worked for the company had ever seen the Owner. He was powerful and successful, yet his conspicuous detachment from day-to-day company matters shrouded the Owner in mystery.

The CEO of the company was a corrupt, small-minded man with a huge ego. Even though the company had been suffering under his leadership, he wanted to run things like the little dictator he was. But the Owner never communicated with him, so the CEO never knew where he stood. Instead, the Owner kept in contact with a junior executive. This infuriated the CEO.

The Owner eventually had enough of the CEO's management style and defiant attitude, so he asked the junior executive to confront him at the next board meeting. He wanted to know how many of the board members were loyal to the Owner, and how many were loyal to the CEO.

The CEO was excited when he heard about the Owner's strategy. Finally he had a chance to take over the company. If he could convince the entire board to side with him, the company would be his for the taking. He had already built a strong executive alliance. His only concern was the junior executive, a charismatic, young man who could be very persuasive.

There was great interest on the part of the board members as well. Most of them were as power-hungry as the CEO. The way they figured it, an alliance with the CEO would mean more for them. Because of the unusual interest in this critical meeting (some were calling it "the Showdown"), the CEO decided to hold it in a conference center in the mountains. The CEO thought the meeting would be over quickly. He would give the junior executive a chance to speak, they would take a vote, badda bing, and it would all be over. The CEO was confident of victory, leaving the Owner in a weakened position. Perhaps the Owner would even be forced to hand the company over. A wry smile crossed the CEO's face as the meeting began.

The junior executive spoke first, and immediately he asked for a vote of confidence for the Owner. "How long are you people going to waver in your loyalty?" he asked. "It's time to choose between the one who built this company and the one who's trying to take it over." He then turned to the board members, who were glaring at him. "Go ahead. Tell everyone about your CEO's accomplishments. Let everyone know how he has squandered the profits and abused our customers."

One by one the board members looked at the CEO. With one voice they asked him to respond. They were expecting the CEO to deliver a clever and creative presentation, but the CEO hadn't anticipated that the focus would be on his actions rather than the Owner's absence. The CEO had nothing to say in his own defense. He knew the junior executive was right. He *was* a lousy leader—and a corrupt one at that.

The board members pleaded with the CEO to make his case, but he didn't say a word. As the color drained from his face, so did his confidence.

"I thought as much," the junior executive said. "Now it's my turn. Let me tell you what the Owner has done for you, the company, and our customers." The junior executive proceeded to boldly explain the Owner's accomplishments. Using a dazzling array of video, sound, and special effects, the junior executive presented the Owner's case. Then the junior executive delivered a message from the Owner: "As of this moment, everyone on the board is through. In fact, anyone loyal to the CEO is gone as of this moment. You're all fired." Then he turned to the CEO. "For some reason, the Owner has decided to keep you on," he told him. "Don't ask me why. The Owner has a plan to grow the company, and he's willing to let you lead."

It was a small victory. The CEO outwardly celebrated at a banquet that night, but inside he was seething. Instead of appreciating his job, the CEO plotted for a way to destroy the junior executive. Even though his allies were all gone, he started making threats.

You would think that the junior executive, fresh from his boardroom victory, wouldn't be concerned in the least about the CEO. But for some reason, he became sick with worry. Even though the junior executive had the full support of the Owner, he felt betrayed and alone. He should have been confident, but the CEO's actions had unnerved him. Quietly he slipped away from the banquet, placed his resignation on the CEO's desk, and drove away into the night. He felt like a total failure.

The preceding tale is true. It happened in 874 B.C. in the Middle East. We didn't use the actual names of the people involved because we didn't want you to know that it's a story from the Bible. You can look it up for yourself in 1 Kings 18:1–19:18. There you will find that in our little story the Owner is God, the company is the Kingdom of Israel, the CEO is King Ahab, the board members are the prophets of Baal, and the junior executive is the prophet Elijah.

Our point isn't to give you a history lesson but to show you that over thousands of years, things don't really change all that much. Oh, technology may be updated, and the products we sell and the services we provide may change, but human nature remains the same.

Success is fleeting, especially when it comes to the work you do. Just like Elijah, you can be riding high one moment, only to quickly sink to the depths of discouragement, despondency, and depression the next. In other words, just because you're a success today doesn't mean you won't fail tomorrow.

You may never be called to stand single-handedly against forces opposed to God (and then again, you might). You may never be called to take sides in a company showdown (and then again, you might). But here's one thing that's sure to happen. Sometime in your life there will come a time when you will be faced with difficulties in your job, and there will be times when you feel like a failure in your career. So the question is not, "What will you do *if* that happens?" What you have to ask yourself is, "What will you do *when* that happens.?"

Career Path to Nowhere

Maybe you are on a career path, where the problem isn't that people oppose you, but rather that you just don't feel like you're going anywhere. You studied to be a professional widget salesman, and now that you're actually out there selling widgets, you're not so sure that you're on the right track. There are times when you feel like jumping off the track and starting over, but you have obligations to fulfill. You don't just quit in the middle of a career.

Or maybe you got the job of your dreams, and it's failed you. There was recently an article in the *Wall Street Journal* about a thirty-year-old Stanford M.B.A. who rode the wave of riches to a position with a Silicon Valley start-up, only to see his net worth shrink to nothing after the Internet stock freefall. In fact, he was in a worse position at the end than when he started: The stock options he had exercised had plunged in value, yet he was faced with a huge tax bill based on their value when he had optioned them.

The article focused on the young man's situation after his wild ride, which saw him devoting day and night to his business interests. To his credit, he had learned some things from this devastating personal failure. "When your job becomes your life, it also becomes your sense of self-worth," he said. "This has long-term consequences that we only think we can sidestep." And then he said something that has special significance for you as you read this chapter: "I felt like God was telling me, 'I told you so.'"

Does Your Work Matter to God?

Have you ever felt that God was saying "I told you so" after you experienced a personal or professional setback? Do you think it's because God doesn't want you to get rich? Do you ever feel guilty because you're working in a "secular" job rather than doing the "Lord's work" in some kind of full-time ministry? Hey, we've all been there. We all think about stuff like that.

You may be reading this and thinking, "Man, I don't need all this negative talk right now. I haven't even started my career." That's OK. You don't need to be in a "career" in order to experience failure. Let's say you're still trying to decide what you want to do. You've gone to school for a few years (OK, you've been in school so long people are referring to you as a "professional student"), but you still aren't sure about your future career. You are reluctant to make a choice because you're afraid you will make the wrong choice. Bottom line: you're afraid to fail. (Quick review from Chapter 2 ... everybody has this fear.)

Still, you want to make something of yourself. You want to be a success. Ideally, you want to find meaning in some kind of work—the kind of meaning that connects you to a nobler purpose and a higher calling. (And you wouldn't mind making a decent living while you're at it.) Does any of this matter to God? Does he care about what you do, or does he just want you to get by on odd jobs while you volunteer at the Rescue Mission?

What You Do Matters to God

God wants you to devote yourself to something, whether you call it a career, a job, an occupation, or just plain work. Far from being an incidental part of God's plan for the world and for you, work is an integral part of God's design.

The Great American Dream used to revolve around work. People came to this country knowing that they could make something of themselves and secure a future for their family—if they were willing to work.

Today that dream has faded as people try to figure out ways to stop working. Rather than looking forward to a lifetime of work (like our immigrant ancestors), people look for ways to retire early. So they play the stock market, or they try to find a job that will give them a rocket ride to riches.

Unfortunately, these are elusive goals for 99.99 percent of us. The chances of striking it rich through any means other than a lifetime of work are about as remote as winning the lottery.

Now, we're going to assume that you aren't looking for quick riches. You're smarter than that. But you don't want to wind up in a dead-end job. Besides that, you just can't shake the notion that "work" is little more than a four-letter word. You want balance in your life, and you're afraid that work might distract you from the more important things. If that's the case, we want to remind you of something: God worked.

Handmade by God

That's right, the Creator of the universe—the Big Cheese, the Almighty One, the God of the Bible—worked. And he was happy to do it. You don't have to go very far in Scripture to read about it. In the first chapter of Genesis, at the completion of the most ambitious construction project the world has ever seen (that would be creation), the Bible says:

> *Then God looked over all he had made, and he saw that it was excellent in every way.*
>
> GENESIS 1:31

A couple of verses later, the Bible says, "God rested from all his work" (Genesis 2:2). Even God, who can do anything he wants, chose to work, and he liked it.

Bible students sometimes mistakenly believe that God cursed humankind with work because of sin. That's not true. Before man chose to disobey God, thereby bringing sin into the world, God placed him in the Garden of Eden, "to tend and care for it" (Genesis 2:15). Work has always been part of God's design for the world and for us. The only thing that happened was that after the Fall, the nature of work changed—it became a struggle—but it never became a curse. God always intended work to be a benefit for his created beings.

Three Things Work Does for Us

In his book *Christians in the Marketplace*, Bill Hybels writes about the benefits of work. You don't have to be a Christian to appreciate these, but as a Christian you can understand that work is God's gift to us. It is much more than a means to make money; work enhances our sense of personal worth in at least three ways:

Work Gives Us Dignity

Dignity is very big on the list of human emotional needs. Every person—regardless of age, ability, ethnic background, gender, social status, or geographic location—longs for dignity. This is what gives us a proper sense of pride and self-respect. "Dignity is available to every person in every legitimate, worthwhile profession," Hybels writes. A ditchdigger can have just as much dignity as a dentist, as long as he is doing his job to the best of his ability and is being recognized for the good work he does (the same goes for the dentist, by the way). The Book of Proverbs (which has a lot to say about the value of work) puts it this way:

> *Do you see any truly competent workers? They will serve kings rather than ordinary people.*
>
> PROVERBS 22:29

As we traveled across America, we met a lot of people who turned ordinary jobs into extraordinary professions simply because they were truly competent. We rode in a cab in New Orleans that was so clean and refreshing (this is very unusual for any cab, especially one in the Big Easy) that we felt like kings being escorted in a limo. The cab driver took great pride in his work, and it gave him great dignity.

Work Helps Us Develop Responsibility

Having a job has an interesting effect on people. It makes them responsible! We watched this principle apply directly to our own daughters recently, and it was almost like witnessing a miracle. Our daughters graduated from college in the spring of the same year (although from different schools), and each of them decided to seek employment during the summer. They found jobs related to their majors (this always makes a father feel good) and entered the workforce at the same time. This gave us an opportunity to compare notes on how they were doing.

Without going into great detail, we'll just say that the biggest change from college to actual work came in the form of responsibility. No longer could our daughters sleep late when they wanted to or skip class when they felt like it. Each of their jobs required that they be there at a certain time and work for a certain number of hours. Neither of them got a job where they had to punch a clock, but it was expected that they be at the office when everyone else got there, mainly because they were now working with a team rather than on their own. As with any team, things work a lot better when everyone shows up.

For the first time in their young lives, our daughters had to be disciplined in the way they arranged their personal schedules. Not only that, but the expectations of their bosses and the competition of the workplace meant that they had to perform to a certain level. They also realized that they must take responsibility for getting ahead in their respective professions.

Work Gives Us a Sense of Accomplishment
There's no feeling like completing a job well done. It doesn't matter if you've just washed your car or completed a complicated report for your supervisor. It feels good to finish a job and to know you did it well. This is true both for individual accomplishments and for achievements that are made as part of a team. Even superstar athletes have said that individual honors pale in comparison to team victories.

Did you know that this sense of accomplishment comes from God? Look back at Genesis 1:31. After completing the task of creating the universe (how's that for a project?), God stepped back and took pride in what he had done.

God Is Your Partner

In Chapter 7, we're going to talk about finances. As a part of that discussion, we're also going to touch on the subject of stewardship and tithing. At the risk of preempting ourselves, we need to make a statement that relates directly to this chapter:

When you give a portion of your resources to God, you aren't giving him a portion of what you own. You are giving him a portion of what he owns. This applies to your time as well as your finances.

In *The Fourth Frontier: Exploring the New World of Work*, Stephen Graves and Thomas Addington write:

Stewardship does not stop—or even start—with giving God a 10 percent stake in our bucks. A more accurate picture, in fact, would look like this: God has totally funded our working life's bank account with 100 percent of the venture capital.

We like the way they put that. It makes you think of life and work as a partnership with God, only God is the Senior Partner. We've got a friend who owns a successful tuxedo rental business called The Best Man. For years he has given each person who rents a tuxedo a card with the following message:

Thank you for allowing us to be of service to you on this occasion.

May we take this opportunity to tell you a little about us. Management has determined to make God the Senior Partner. In a crisis, the problem is turned over to Him, and He never fails to help us with the answer. Each of our services must reflect the integrity of management, including our Senior Partner. If sometimes we fail because we are human, we find it imperative to do our utmost to make it right.

Besides being our Senior Partner, He is our Heavenly Father. In Him we find security in troubled times. If you are perplexed or troubled and are looking for answers, may we invite you to look to Him. God loves you.

If you feel that you would like to talk to someone or want someone to pray with you, please feel free to call us.

That's the attitude God wants you to have at your work, whether you own a business or work for someone else. As Graves and Addington put it: "Our work matters to God. It cannot save us, but it is of value. As stewards, ones entrusted with assets, we are responsible for what we do and more important, how we do it. We are to serve God's purposes, giving him glory and serving others."

If you are frustrated with your work, or you feel like you're failing at what you do, perhaps you need to see your work or your career from an entirely new perspective. Rather than doing your work your way with the results you want, think of doing God's work God's way with the results God wants.

Work As a Calling

"I received the call to ministry when I was a junior in college." We were talking with a respected college professor about his work as an educator. He was teaching in a Christian college, working with students in profound and life-changing ways, yet he was restless. He had this strong sense that he had turned his back on ministry.

"But you minister to students every single day," we reminded him.

"I know, but I can't help but think that I have turned my back on my calling," he said. We were puzzled, until we talked further and realized that in the mind of this gifted teacher, the "call to minister" was the same as being called to be a minister, and that meant being a minister in a church. Even though he was serving God full time as a Christian college professor, he believed his true call was to the church.

This got us to thinking about the true nature of "the call." No doubt you've heard ministers or pastors say they received "the call to preach" when they were very young. Maybe a missionary stood up in your church and talked about being "called to the mission field." Have you ever wondered what that was all about? What is "the call" anyway? Is it some mysterious divine tap on the shoulder that comes only to those souls worthy of the task of serving God in "full-time Christian ministry?" Are the rest of us second-class spiritual citizens who merely do the world's work rather than God's?

We happen to believe that there is a very special calling to serve God as a pastor, a priest, a missionary, or an evangelist. These are unique positions that require unique gifts. People in these roles are called to be our spiritual leaders, and we are to treat them with respect as such (see Hebrews 13:7). Yet only a few, relative to the total population of this earth, are called to serve God in this way. It is much more likely that you will be called to serve God in other ways, such as teaching, business, medicine, government, communications, or technology. God may be calling you to be involved in sports or the arts. You may serve God best by serving your country in the armed forces.

The point is that all of us are called by God to serve him in whatever job, vocation, or career he has gifted us to do. You're not a failure if you don't serve God in full-time Christian ministry—if that's not what God has called you to do. Failure comes when you refuse to invite God to be the Senior Partner in the work he has called you to do.

In his book, *Business As a Calling*, Michael Novak says that two things are necessary for you to identify God's call for you:

1. God has given you the ability to do the job.
2. God has given you enjoyment in doing it.

Remember the movie *Chariots of Fire?* Eric Liddel was a gifted athlete who believed that God gave him the ability to run fast. Against the advice of his sister, who felt he should serve God as a missionary, Eric trained so he could compete in the Olympics. "When I run I feel his pleasure," Eric told his sister, referring to the enjoyment God gave him when he ran. Eric eventually became a missionary, but not before he did the job God gave him to do.

Four Characteristics of a Calling

Michael Novak lists four qualities you should be looking for as you try to determine what God wants you to do. Notice how all of these revolve around your God-given ability and enjoyment:

Each calling is unique . That's because each of us is made uniquely in God's image. God's image is infinite just as God is infinite. St. Thomas Aquinas once wrote that it would take an infinite number of human beings to reflect the "infinite facets" of God. So don't worry about all the good jobs being taken. There's plenty to do for the person willing to serve God whole-heartedly.

A calling requires preconditions. Each of us has certain abilities, physical gifts, mental horsepower, and personality traits. God won't call you to do some-thing he hasn't given you the ability to do.

A true calling results in enjoyment. If you hate what you do, don't blame the job. Maybe you aren't called to do it. According to Novak, you will know if you are called to do something when you become energized in the process of doing it.

A calling is not always easy to discover. One of the greatest gifts God gives to each of us is freedom. God could have created us as little robots pro-grammed to obey him at all times. But what enjoyment would God take in that? And what enjoyment would we find in doing something about which we had no choice? Freedom to choose is a wonderful thing, but it is also fraught with peril. (It's not often we get to use the phrase "fraught with peril," and we're not sure we used it correctly here, but you have to admit that it sounds good.) Along with the freedom to make the right choices comes the freedom to make the wrong ones. When it comes to your work, you may have to wade through a few jobs and maybe even a career or two before you find something you feel God has called you to do.

Does Your Call Ever Change?

The call of God seems like such a permanent thing. Does it ever change? Absolutely. The Bible is full of people who changed careers. Joseph changed careers from a shepherd to a ruler of Egypt. A simple Jewish woman, Esther went on to become the queen of Persia. Luke changed jobs from a physician to a biographer. In our own time, exam-ples are everywhere. Millard Fuller was a lawyer, and then he got involved in a little building project called Habitat for Humanity. Don't think of any job or career as permanent. Your work is merely the vehi-cle through which God will use you to impact and influence others.

A calling won't undermine the other important things in your life. Mr. Novak didn't say this, but we want to make it a point. By "other important things" we mean your family, your health, and your personal walk with God. We've seen many people—and so have you—who were convinced they were doing what God called them to do, even though their own families were suffering from neglect. We've seen others who were working so hard for the Lord that their health suffered irreparable harm. And then in the irony of all ironies, we know from personal experience that it's possible to get so caught up in doing what God wants you to do that you neglect your own daily, personal relationship with him.

Do you think God would call you to do something that would damage your relationships, your health, or your walk with him? Not on your life. God wants you to keep your life in balance, which isn't an easy thing. That's why he offers to help you.

How God Helps

We want to close this chapter by getting back to our friend Elijah. When we last left this great man of God, he had fled in fear from a king he had just humiliated. Elijah was huddled beneath a scraggly tree, wanting in the worst way for God to take his life (see 1 Kings 19:3-4). The Bible doesn't say this, but we get the mental picture of a guy curled up in a fetal position, his thumb firmly planted in his mouth (hey, don't laugh, we've all been there). Our good friend Chuck Swindoll writes this about Elijah at this stage of his life:

1. He was not thinking realistically or clearly.
2. He had separated himself from strengthening relationships.
3. He was caught in the backwash of a great victory.
4. He was physically exhausted and emotionally spent.
5. He got lost in self-pity.

Can you identify with this? We sure can. Sometimes the failure you feel in a job you have just completed or a career you have chosen is due in large part to one or more of these five factors. When you feel alone, or you're exhausted from completing a very important task, or you are emotionally spent even though you have done the job well, you can easily get to the point where you feel your life isn't worth spit. You may not feel like taking your own life, but like Elijah, you wouldn't mind it so much if God decided to take you home right there and then. At the very least, you set the table for your very own pity party.

When you find yourself in this situation, there's really only one thing to do. You need to go to God for help. Ask him to bring you back to life. Allow God to get you over your feelings of failure. We're not saying that God is going to make you feel like a dragon slayer again (at least not right away), but he will restore your joy and your resolve. To get a picture of what God will do when you find yourself in Elijah's position, read 1 Kings 19:5-21. Dr. Swindoll analyzed this passage of Scripture and came up with three things God did for Elijah.

God allowed Elijah a time of rest and refreshment. Rest is highly undervalued in our culture, yet it is badly needed. Even God rested from his work of creation (see Genesis 2:2). If God took a day off, what makes us think we can get by without doing the same? R.C. Sproul once told the story of a golf course that was traditionally closed on Mondays so the fairways and greens would have a chance to rest and recover after six days of constant play. In an effort to bring in more revenue, the course owners decided to open the course on Mondays to private parties and special groups.

It wasn't long before the course started looking tattered and abused. The regular members complained and several dropped their membership, resulting in a net loss of dollars, even with the added income on Mondays. The same principle applies to each of us. We can't burn the candle on both ends and expect life to keep going. Something's got to give. Not only is rest a practical way to recover from your work, it is God's design for your life.

God communicated wisely with Elijah. King David wrote: "Be silent and know that I am God!" (Psalm 46:10). Because our lives are so noisy and cluttered, we expect God to shout his way into our hearts and minds. Sometimes he gets our attention from some pretty big things, but more often than not God operates quietly. The only way we can hear him is to slow down and listen for his voice. God came to Elijah—not in a windstorm, an earthquake, or a fire—but in a "gentle whisper" (1 Kings 19:12). Is God whispering to you? You won't know until you chase the noise out of your life.

God gave Elijah a close, personal friend. This is one of the greatest gifts God will ever give you. King Solomon wrote: "A real friend sticks closer than a brother" (Proverbs 18:24). It's true! There's nothing like a loyal friend to encourage you and see you through challenging times. If you're feeling like a failure, maybe you lack a close, personal friend. God introduced Elijah to Elisha, and the two made an effective team. We can tell you from personal experience that a close friendship is more than pleasant; it's powerful.

A Final Word About Your Career Path and Success

There are two ways to approach a job, a career, or even a special project. The first way is to find something that appeals to you and matches up with your abilities, and then do that. Oh, and while you're at it, you can ask God to bless what you're doing. It may work for you. And then again, it may be frustrating, unfulfilling, and exhausting.

The second way is to follow the advice of Henry Blackaby and Claude King in their phenomenal best-seller, *Experiencing God.* In a nutshell, the authors suggest that success will come when you first find what God is doing, and then join him. Then you are sure to experience God and a life that is meaningful, fulfilling, and exciting.

Remember, it's not easy, but it is incredibly rewarding.

Moving on to Money

It would be nice if you could choose a job or a career strictly on the basis of how much you enjoy it and how meaningful it is. Yet there's another factor that enters into almost everything you do, and that's money. Don't kid yourself. As much as you'd like to believe that you're not motivated by money, it occupies a great deal of your time. When you're not working to earn it, you're wondering how you can make more. You're not greedy; you're practical. You don't want to get rich; you want to be comfortable.

So how come money is such a big issue? In Chapter 7 we're going to talk about money and you and why you struggle from time to time (OK, so maybe you struggle a lot). We're going to take the mystique out of money so you can minimize your mistakes.

> I know of nothing more despicable and pathetic
> than a man who devotes all the hours of the
> waking day to the making of money
> for money's sake.

—John D. Rockefeller

CHAPTER 7

When Your Financial Dream
Turns Into a Nightmare

If you are like most people, you spend about 50 percent of your time thinking about money. Of course, that includes all of the time you devote to:

A. Earning it;

B. Saving it;

C. Spending it; and

D. Worrying about not having enough of it (because you are much better at "C" than either "A" or "B").

And, unless you are still living on a parental subsidy (commonly known as an "allowance"), or have traded in your Ralph Lauren designer labels for the austerity of Amish apparel, you are living in a financially oriented reality.

You can't escape the world of high finance. You log onto the Internet and find a "ten simple steps to avoid your creditors" article on your homepage.

You run on the treadmill at the gym and the fifteen televisions in the room are all tuned to either the "Financial News Network" or "Wall Street Week" on PBS. You browse the magazine racks at the supermarket checkout stand, and find articles about everything from reducing your income taxes to investing in real estate to the *National Enquirer*'s headline story about an outer-space alien who serves as the financial planner for Kathy Lee.

In our society, it is easy to get caught up in acquiring more money, bigger houses, and better toys. Somewhere along the line our culture shifted its philosophy from "having enough" to "getting more."

This shift in mentality can be seen by contrasting the wisdom of Ben Franklin (from his *Poor Richard's Almanack*) with our contemporary vernacular expressions. It doesn't take a linguist or Alan Greenspan to see that society has gotten more aggressive and possessive when it comes to money:

In the Era of Ben Franklin:	In the Era of Donald Trump:
Early to bed, early to rise, makes a man healthy, wealthy, and wise.	You have to pay the price.
The early bird catches the worm.	You snooze, you lose.
A penny saved is a penny earned.	The one with all the toys wins.

When people get caught up in this quest-to-possess mentality, they get thrown off balance and lose their economic equilibrium. You'll know when you have become part of this group, your fiscal life will be turned inside-out:

> ## If your outgo exceeds your income, your upkeep will be your downfall.

Once you buy into our culture's success syndrome, it can be very easy to feel like a financial failure if you can't immediately achieve what you have set out to accomplish. Let's face it, if your *real life* falls far short of what society says it ought to be, then it is hard to feel good about yourself. Take this little test to see if you are suffering from feelings of financial failure:

- Are you trying your best to convince everyone that you are keeping up financially although you are really falling behind?

- Do you keep checking the mail box for a new credit card application because you are maxed out on the ones you have?

- Has your bank offered to give you a "speed dial" button on the ATM because you are such a frequent user?

- Did you gamble on the NASDAQ and come up a big loser by socking all of your money into Pets.com, leaving you with nothing but your socks?

- Are you counting on the inefficiency of the U.S. Postal Service because you need a few days to put money in your checking account to cover the checks that you have already mailed?

- Are you spending money you don't have to buy things you don't need to impress people you don't even like?

- When you tell people that you have a six-figure balance in your investment account, are two of those figures on the right side of the decimal point?

If you answered "yes" to any of these questions, there is a good chance that you've got money problems. But don't despair. Your situation is not fatal. Whether you are just disappointed because you haven't accumulated the wealth that you desire, or whether you are anemic and your health is in jeopardy because you have been selling your blood to make your rent payments, your situation can improve. And it can improve immediately. You can put yourself on the road to financial success today, if you choose to do so. It is just a matter of:

Assessment

Attitude

Action

It will take all three to get you going in the right direction. But it can happen. This doesn't mean that you will end up with more dollars, but you'll definitely end up with more sense.

If you learn to live within your income, you'll be living without a lot of things ... and worry will be one of them.

Assessment: Is the Problem With Your Earning or Your Yearning?

If you are serious about slipping out of the financial noose, you've got to see what got you hung up in the first place. Self-examination can be a painful experience because you may not like what you see. Staring in a mirror now is better than staring in the face of a bankruptcy judge later. (If the sight of Judge Judy makes you wince, then you are likely to get nauseous in the presence of a bankruptcy judge.)

How Did You Get Into This Mess?

This is a legitimate question, but you've got to answer it honestly or there is no sense in asking it. Your initial response may be to blame circumstances that are beyond your control. ("I'd be doing great if the stock market hadn't gone down. Who could have ever expected that to happen?") Or maybe you'll be tempted to blame other people. ("It's all my grandmother's fault. She shouldn't have wasted my future inheritance on those medical expenses. That ventilator was an extravagance that used up money I was counting on.") But the problem isn't other people or other circumstances. The problem is you. (Sorry for being blunt about it.) While everyone's situation is different, the cause of your financial failure may fall into one of several very common categories:

You Earn Too Little

Everyone would like to be paid more. But usually your compensation is commensurate with the value of your service to your employer. Or at least it is dictated by similar jobs in the marketplace. You may need more money to live on, but if you are working the drive-thru window at Fat Burger, your employer can't justify paying you an annual salary of $100,000 (no matter how reliable, competent, and friendly you are).

Minimum-wage jobs are a great starting place, but you will be forever frustrated financially if you stay at that level. If you aren't working at a job that pays a wage that is realistic for your circumstances (more about realism below), then you need to plan to take a few steps up on the financial food chain (and we aren't referring to moving up from Fat Burger to the drive-thru window of a more prestigious fast-food franchise).

You Spend Too Much

This may be the fly in your financial soup. You make enough money to live on, but you are spending more than you make. That's called deficit spending. Who do you think you are, the government? The government can spend more than it collects because it has the ability to raise taxes and print more money. But you probably can't raise your own salary, and printing your own money is illegal. (Although you'll get free room and board in prison, and fifteen to twenty years in a cell may curb your spending habits.)

The Social Security Administration
has reported that 97% of the population
spend 3 to 15% more than they make.

You can get by for a little while if you are going in the hole each month, but before long you'll be so far in debt that you can't recover. The interest charges on your credit cards and loans will consume all of your discretionary income. Before long you'll be unable to purchase those extravagant items that you have become so fond of ... like food and utilities. If you are spending more than you are making, you will be building a molehill of debt into a mountain of problems.

Debt is like quicksand.
You'll walk right into it unless you watch where
you're going, and once you're in it, you'll have a
tough time getting out.

You Neglect to Put Anything Away for a Rainy Day

Maybe you read the preceding paragraph with a smug attitude because you have been disciplined enough in your spending to avoid debt. You don't spend one penny more than you make. But now you are in trouble because you don't spend one penny less than you make either. You spend your entire salary each month, and never sock anything away for a rainy day. "Why should I?" you think. "I'm young, I'm healthy, and I lead a charmed life. Nothing bad is going to happen to me."

Everyone thinks that way at first. Then, with a clap of thunder, a torrential downpour of financial misfortune floods your life. The timing belt breaks on your car. The bad news is that you need to buy a new car. The good news is that you don't need one to commute to work because your company downsized and now you are out of a job. Then you discover that you can't stay at home because your apartment building is converting to condos, and you've got to move out in a month. If you've never saved anything out of your paycheck, you have no financial reserves. That makes it difficult to put down the first and last months' rent on a new apartment and the down payment on a new car....

Now, you can borrow the money you need. After all, isn't that the purpose of cash advances on your credit cards? The trouble is, once you have a new job, you still won't have enough money to support your lifestyle because much of your income will be disbursed in the payment of interest charges. You'll be spending more than you ever anticipated for interest and debt reduction (since you previously anticipated "zero" for these items). With the loan payments and your usual living expenses, you'll probably be spending more than you are earning (which assumes you get a new job). You've got debt dead ahead in your future. Now go back and re-read the preceding paragraph to see what you're in for (and this time you won't be so smug).

What's the Real Reason for Your Financial Failings?

More money won't solve your problems. Oh, it might help for a little while. (At least you can pay off the loan shark, stop moving money between checking accounts in an attempt to avoid bouncing checks, redeem your grandfather's wheelchair from the pawn shop, and cancel the plan to sell your kidney.) Yet you are likely to find yourself back in the same situation unless you come to grips with the feelings about money that got you there in the first place.

Everybody has feelings toward money. The wrong feelings can get you into trouble.

- If you are indifferent about it, then you won't be keeping track of how much you've got or where it goes. Money can't buy happiness, but it does pay the bills, so you need to give some attention to your financial situation.
- If you are possessive of it, then you will be either hoarding your money or spending to buy possessions that you can accumulate. Remember that money is not the root of all evil. It is the *love* of money that is fatal.
- If you are too permissive with it, you won't spend it properly. When you acquire it, you will say "hello" and then you will kiss it "goodbye." You won't use it productively, and then it won't be around to do you any good when you need it.

According to a 1980 report by the U.S. Department of Human Resources, only 3% of the population reach age 65 and are financially independent:
  29% die before reaching age 65.
  13% reach that age but are below the poverty level.
  55% are in the middle group with the median income of $6,800 per year.
  3% have incomes over $29,000 per year (which didn't buy much even in 1980).

> **Money is like friendship. You have to work hard to earn it, but it can be easily thrown away.**

Before we move to the next section of this chapter that examines the proper attitude toward money, let's consider some of the perspectives that might have caused your financial failures of the past:

- *Procrastination.* This is often the number one culprit in financial failures. People just put off doing something about their situation. They don't expend extra effort to get a better-paying job (although they intend to get around to it someday). They know they should stop overspending, but they don't want to miss the "Once-In-a-Lifetime Sale Extravaganza" at the neighborhood department store (which is held on the first weekend of every month). And they know they should establish a savings account, so they are starting the process of getting ready to begin to prepare to start thinking about doing something about it at some as yet unspecified date in the not too distant future.

You've Got a Sordid Past

We aren't talking about that episode on your police record that involved a break-in at the college chemistry lab and a subsequent stink bomb at a nearby dormitory. We're talking about your credit report.

If you have had financial difficulties in the past, then your credit report is like an ominous cloud of financial despair that floats above you wherever you go. You won't be approved for new credit cards if you have defaulted on previous ones. You won't get approved for a home loan if you have a history of paying your bills late. And if you are lucky enough to get approved for a loan of any kind, it is only because you're dealing with a loan shark who is charging interest at an exorbitant rate.

A bad credit report is like a public announcement that you are a financial loser. It will haunt you wherever you go. Life is difficult when someone runs a computerized credit check on you and speakers start blaring "Alert! Alert!" while there is an image on the monitor screen of a cartoon caricature flushing money down a toilet with a caption that reads: "Don't let this happen to you!"

> The road to the bankruptcy court is paved
> with the good intentions of those who knew what
> they should be doing.

- *Failure to Have a Plan.* Many people don't bother setting financial goals. They live in ignorant bliss—for a while. You never feel bad about missing the target if you aren't aiming at anything. Yet the absence of a plan can spell disaster when you are unprepared to handle unexpected financial emergencies (like the loss of a job or a medical emergency). These setbacks make you feel bad enough; without a financial cushion, you'll feel even worse! You can anticipate some financial transitions, such as purchasing a house, feeding the kids, and your own retirement. But you need to make a plan—and stick to it—*now*. If you don't have a plan for handling the foreseeable and unanticipated expenses that will surely suck the cash from your wallet, you will suffer financially your entire life.

> No one plans to fail. They just fail to plan.

- *Ignorance about financial matters.* Don't be offended. We aren't suggesting you might be ignorant. We are just saying that you might not be knowledgeable about money. It is a complex subject. Successful management of your finances requires knowledge about investments, income taxes, and budgeting. If you haven't learned the basics, then you can get caught in some costly traps.

To move yourself from financial failure to success may require that you abandon your previous financial habits. That will be easier to do if you make sure that you have a proper perspective about money. We're going to suggest that "who it belongs to" and "how you handle it" are topics that have a spiritual dimension.

Attitude: Whose Money Is It?

You came into the world with nothing, and you aren't going to take anything with you when you go. What makes you think that the assets that you get in the time between the snipping of your umbilical cord and the closing of your casket belong to you?

The Bible has an interesting perspective on finances. It says that everything belongs to God.

> *The earth is the Lord's, and everything in it. The world and all its people belong to him.*
>
> PSALM 24:1

> *Riches and honor come from you alone, for you rule over everything.... Everything we have has come from you, and we give you only what you have already given us!*
>
> 1 CHRONICLES 29:12, 14

However, the I.R.S. certainly doesn't adhere to this position. It requires income taxes from you (not to mention that annoying F.I.C.A. withholding) because your name is on the paycheck. So where do *you* fit into the "God owns everything" scenario? We can answer that question with one word: *"oikonomos."* Although that sounds like the name of a prescription ointment for athlete's foot fungus, it is a Greek word that translates into English as *stewardship*. The term implies a manager of a household who administers someone else's property. God has made us the stewards of his possessions:

> *You put us in charge of everything you made, giving us authority over all things.*
>
> PSALM 8:6

If what we have belongs to God, then we should manage it according to his principles. This perspective means that every decision we make about our money—from how to spend it to how to invest it—has spiritual ramifications. We are not just accountable to God for the few bucks we might toss into the offering basket at church, and we are not off the hook with God so long as we pay him a surcharge (or in God's case, is it a *Sir* charge?) of a certain percentage of our earnings. If God owns it all, then we must be faithful stewards in handling all of it.

Crown Ministries is an organization devoted to teaching biblical principles of money management. The study materials of Crown Ministries identify the following eight areas in which we should be faithful as financial stewards:

1. *We should work diligently.*
2. *We should spend wisely.*
3. *We should save consistently.*
4. *We should avoid debt.*
5. *We should give generously.*
6. *We should deal with others honestly.*
7. *We should seek wise counsel from others.*
8. *We should teach our children how to manage money properly.*

If you believe the Bible when it says that everything belongs to God, then you can believe the Bible when it says that God will take care of all of our needs. Your part is to be a good steward of what God has given to you; God's part is to make sure that you have everything that you need:

So don't worry about having enough food or drink or clothing. Why be like the pagans who are so deeply concerned about these things? Your heavenly Father already knows all your needs, and he will give you all you need from day to day if you live for him and make the Kingdom of God your primary concern.

MATTHEW 6:31-33

If we approach our finances as belonging to God instead of ourselves, it will make us more responsible in how we handle our money, and it will change our perspectives about what is important in life.

Living With a Sense of Sacred Simplicity

If we handle our finances as if they belong to God, and if we trust him to provide all of our needs, then we don't have to panic when the stock market drops or the price of Oreos at the supermarket rises. God is in charge, and we don't have to worry about our future:

> *Don't worry about anything; instead, pray about everything. Tell God what you need, and thank him for all he has done. If you do this, you will experience God's peace, which is far more wonderful than the human mind can understand. His peace will guard your hearts and minds as you live in Christ Jesus.*
>
> PHILIPPIANS 4:6-7

There is the real secret for shedding feelings of being a financial failure. When you live with a divine perspective about your finances, it simplifies your life. Instead of fretting about your money, you can enjoy a feeling of sacred simplicity. Approaching life with a view of sacred simplicity works something like this:

- *God will supply all of your needs,* so you don't have to worry about them.

- *You can be content with what you have now,* and you can be content in the future if God increases or decreases your net worth. The amount doesn't really matter because God has promised to give you everything you need.

- *You don't need to worry about the future.* There may be times of increase and decrease in your financial position. Either way, God is in charge. In both circumstances you trust him. You don't rely on your cash reserves in the good times, and you don't worry about insufficiency in the tough times.

The concept of sacred simplicity is foreign to our culture. It goes against the prevailing thought of becoming self-sufficient and independently wealthy with a plump 401(k) plan and a fat IRA account. So, it is natural that you might misunderstand the applicable principles of sacred simplicity.

Don't get the wrong impression.

⇒ *Sacred simplicity is not devoted deprivation.* You aren't required to give all of your money to the missionaries. You don't have to cancel Christmas; giving presents to your friends and family is not sinful.

⇒ *Sacred simplicity is not pious parsimony.* God doesn't want you to blame him for being a cheapskate. You don't have to stiff the waitress out of a 15 percent tip and you don't have to sneak soda and treats into the movie theatre just because you are trying to be a good steward of God's money. He wants the waitress to get a generous tip, and he doesn't want you to smuggle Junior Mints in your socks.

⇒ *Sacred simplicity is not ardent austerity.* Good stewardship does not require selling all of your possessions and wearing a trash bag instead of clothes from the Gap. You don't have to sell your 1998 Toyota and replace it with a 1973 Pinto wagon (if you can find a Pinto that is still running). God doesn't object to money or the things that it can buy. But he does want you to have the proper perspective.

⇒ *Sacred simplicity is not sanctimonious sluggishness.* Don't think that you can quit your job and live on the beach because God has promised to provide everything you need. Stewardship requires you to be a diligent worker.

If you want to move from failure to success in your finances, then change your perspective and attitude. Realize that everything belongs to God and that you are responsible to him as a steward for what he has given to you. Then relax and stop worrying because God has everything under control.

Sacred simplicity has nothing to do with the quantity of your money. But it has everything to do with the quality of your heart.

Action: You Can't Climb out of the Hole
If You Keep Digging Deeper!

Your financial problems won't be immediately solved just by identifying your mistakes in the past (making your assessment) and understanding the principles of sacred simplicity (adjusting your attitude). You are going to have to take some action. The assessment and the attitude part will make you feel better, but the action will make your creditors feel better.

The plan of action for each person will be different. We don't know your specific situation, but we are sure it bears some resemblance to circumstances that we have been in from time to time. So, allow us to give you three generic steps for taking action that will make your financial life a successful one.

#1. Extract Yourself From Debt.

This doesn't mean that you shouldn't have a mortgage. (With escalating home prices, you may never be able to save money fast enough by living in an apartment until you can pay cash for a house.) The type of debt you should avoid is an obligation where you lack the actual or potential ability to repay it. This means that you shouldn't take on a car loan if you couldn't cover the loan payment for a few months if you were out of work. And you shouldn't put charges on your credit card if you can't pay off the bill in full at the end of each month.

You probably can't get out of debt all at once, but you should at least begin to make progress on reducing the amount that you owe. As you earn more money (with raises or a second job), don't increase your spending to consume the extra amount. Keep your lifestyle as it is and use the extra amount to pay down on your loans.

#2. Discipline Yourself in Spending.

This may be difficult if you have never tried it before. You might find yourself trying to rationalize purchases that you don't really need. Here are some guidelines to help you resist the compulsion:

- *You don't have to buy something just because it is a "bargain."* A true bargain is a discounted price on something that you need at a time when you can afford it. No matter how low the price is, it is not a bargain if you can't spare the cash to pay for it.

- *Just because the price is discounted doesn't mean that God wants you to have it.* Satan will be glad to arrange a low price for you if it means keeping you in debt.

- *Just because you have the money in your bank account doesn't mean that you have to spend it.* Remember that the balance in your account may have to cover unexpected expenses or routine ones that are just around the corner. (Those tires on your car are looking rather bald. They will need to be replaced soon.)

Before You Buy... Ask Yourself:

1. **What is the real reason that I want to make this purchase?**
   Don't make the purchase if your answer has anything to do with peer pressure, envy, or self-esteem.
2. **What is the standard of living that God wants me to maintain?**
   Don't be tempted to exceed that lifestyle once you have reached it.

#3. Start Giving Generously.

At first glance, giving to your church and other charitable organizations may seem to be counterproductive to controlling your spending. But remember, you are handling God's money. Giving to others may help you acknowledge God's priority in your finances. It might take you a little longer to get out of debt, but the principle of stewardship doesn't depend on making you as comfortable as possible as soon as possible.

Giving might be a new experience for you. If it is, here are a few pointers to help you get started:

- *Your giving should be systematic.* Do it on a regular basis. Make it a habit.

- *Your giving should be sacrificial.* Don't just give out of your excess or in an amount that is insignificant to you. Make your financial gifts a significant part of your budget.

- *Your giving should be spontaneous.* Don't be reluctant to make a gift at the time you see a need. Let God guide you, and don't be inappropriately restrained by your calendar or your traditions.

- *Your giving should be spiritual.* Don't base all of your giving on whether or not it is tax deductible. Be open to God guiding your decisions. God may want you to give financial assistance to someone you know (whose tire tread may be lower than yours), even though there is no place on your 1040 tax form for deducting "spending $100 to help the widow who lives next door to me."

What Motivates You?

Financial failures typically have one thing in common: a selfish motivation. The financial area of our lives gets out of control when it is the source of our motivation. Debt and overspending are usually the result of selfish perspective.

If you can change your perspective about your finances, you can change your financial situation. You can move from failure to success by assessing how you got into your current circumstances, by taking the attitude of a steward who can live in sacred simplicity, and then taking deliberate action to handle your finances properly.

Choices, Choices, Choices

So far in this book we have been talking about changing your perspective about failure (by looking at the upside success potential) and changing your attitude. We have asked you to check your motivation and to make a few adjustments in your daily routine. Yet even if you do all of those things, you may still get bogged down in the mire of failure if you can't make decisions that put you on the road to success.

Decisions can make or break you. If you have had poor experience with your own decisions in the past, don't let that discourage you. You can start making better decisions by following a few simple guidelines.

If you are anxious to leave poor decisions behind you and get a fresh start, begin by making the decision to turn the page.

> People whose lives are affected by
> a decision must be part of the process of
> arriving at that decision.
>
> —John Naisbitt

CHAPTER 8

When Your Good Judgment Fails You

In September 1991, a crew of six men set out from Gloucester, Massachusetts, on a 72-foot fishing boat called the *Andrea Gail*. There was nothing extraordinary about the crew, the boat, or their captain, Billy Tyne. Fishing is the business of the coastal towns of New England, and it was Captain Tyne's business to bring back a substantial catch of swordfish from the fertile waters of the North Atlantic.

Billy Tyne had a knack for finding fish, but on this particular trip, scheduled to last no more than a month, his catch was mediocre at best. Captain Tyne had traveled 1,200 miles out of Gloucester to the Grand Banks, and his crew had caught barely enough to pay expenses, let alone enjoy a fat paycheck themselves. So the *Andrea Gail* pressed on to the Flemish Cap, farther than Tyne liked to go. His strategy paid off when his crew hauled in a boatload of swordfish—60,000 pounds to be exact. Now it was a matter of heading home with their valuable cargo, resting on ice in the ship's hold below.

There was only one problem. Through a meteorological oddity that occurs once in a hundred years, three forces of nature converged in one region to create a storm of epic proportions. Even before the triple threat fully developed, experts were calling it the Storm of the Century. Several years later, Sebastian Junger wrote about it in a best-selling book, *The Perfect Storm*. This storm lay directly between the *Andrea Gail* and Gloucester. Every other boat in the area near the storm either sailed around it or waited it out at a safe distance. Not the *Andrea Gail*.

No one will ever know for certain why Billy Tyne decided to risk his life and the lives of his men to sail back to Gloucester through the heart of the "perfect storm." However, Junger was able to piece together all of the factors, circumstances, and psychological profiles he could find into a story as dramatic as the storm itself.

What is known for sure is that Tyne and his crew were strongly motivated to return to Gloucester rather than waiting out the storm, primarily because the ice machine on their boat had ceased to function. The entire load of fish was in danger of spoiling if they didn't get back home as scheduled. As he interviewed the townspeople who had known and worked with Billy Tyne, Junger also learned that the boat captain was determined, stubborn, and more than a little anxious for a big payday. Whatever combination of factors—the malfunctioning ice machine, financial pressures, overconfidence, lack of information—the captain and crew of the *Andrea Gail* made a fateful decision.

If you've read the book or seen the movie (with George Clooney as Billy Tyne), then you know what happened. After valiantly fighting 120 mph winds and ten-story waves, the *Andrea Gail* finally capsized, and all aboard were lost at sea. It was an unimaginable tragedy for the friends and family of the six seamen and the citizens of Gloucester, made even more tragic by the fact that it could have been avoided—if the captain's judgment had not failed him. Most likely the fish would have been lost, but the lives of six men would have been saved.

Join the Club

We've all made bad decisions in our lives. If you're reading this, then at the very least you haven't yet made a decision that cost you your life (are we perceptive, or what?). If you are reading this book in prison, then you've made some bad decisions for which you are suffering the consequences (but at least you're alive). If you are reading this in a mountain hideaway with a sack full of money buried beneath your cabin, then you have made some bad decisions for which you haven't yet paid the price (but at least you're not in prison yet).

Chances are that none of these situations apply to you. But if you're living, breathing, and reading, then we know you have made your share of bad decisions. Your judgment has failed you more times than you care to remember. The reason we can say this with such confidence is that you're no different than we are. We're all human, and we've all made mistakes. Bad mistakes. But somehow we're still here. We're writing and you're reading, which puts us in a cozy little relationship, at least for now.

So, let's learn from our mistakes. Before this book on failure (and success) goes any further, let's find out how to avoid bad judgment and make good decisions.

You'll never live long enough to make all the mistakes yourself, so learn from the mistakes of others.

Why Make Good Decisions?

OK, we admit that this seems like a dumb question. After all, who in their right mind deliberately makes bad decisions? Well, we can think of at least two people, and their initials are B and S.

The truth is, good people deliberately make bad decisions all the time. There are lots of reasons for this:

✓ Some people deliberately make bad decisions because they don't care about the consequences.

✓ Some people make bad decisions because they don't think the rules apply to them, and they are equally certain about getting around the consequences.

✓ Some people don't realize they are making a bad decision at first – only in retrospect, when they finally have all the facts in front of them.

We're going to assume that you fall into the third category ... most of the time. So what we need to do is figure out why good decisions make more sense than bad decisions.

The way we look at it, you shouldn't spend your time worrying about failing because you make the wrong decisions. That would be like our friend Karl Wallenda in Chapter 2, who died thinking about not falling. Instead, let's concentrate on learning how to succeed by making good decisions.

> **Making good decisions is not about avoiding failure ... it's all about building success.**

Making Good Decisions: How Hard Can It Be?

Unless your mother dropped you on your head when you were a child, or you spent your high school years sniffing glue, you are probably a normal person, faced with normal decisions every day of your life:

✓ Deciding between regular or extra crispy
✓ Choosing the friends you want to hang out with
✓ Deciding what classes to take in school
✓ Determining which job to take when you get out of school
✓ Deciding if you want to get married
✓ Wondering who you should marry

✓ Deciding if you should rent or buy
✓ Choosing the church you want to attend
✓ Deciding whether to have children

Obviously, some of your decisions have few (if any) long-term consequences. Others will affect you for a while, and some have huge implications for your life. But when you average out the decisions you make in the course of your day, your year, and your life, it would seem like a pretty straightforward process.

So why does the decision-making process often seem like walking through a minefield? If experience is the best teacher, why is it so hard to make good decisions? Why do we avoid some seemingly trivial decisions like the plague, while we hastily make more important decisions rather than take our time?

In their book, *How to Make the Right Decisions,* John Arnold and Bert Tompkins list five reasons why decision making is so tough:

✓ *We hope the situation will resolve itself and not require a decision.* Rather than accept the fact that a decision is necessary, we may distance ourselves from the problem and simply refuse to make a decision. Like the proverbial ostrich that sticks his head in the ground, we act like a problem doesn't exist if we can't see it.

✓ *We are unwilling to take responsibility.* Making a decision causes us to become responsible for the outcome, so there will be times when we just don't want to get that involved. We have all heard about the tragic case of the woman who was beaten and raped in her own apartment. Her neighbors heard her cries, but didn't act decisively because they were unwilling to get involved.

✓ *We have too many choices.* In our culture, the difficulty of decision making is often compounded by the overwhelming number of choices available for any one situation. Have you thought about buying a computer lately? You've got to make a hundred decisions just to purchase a simple device that will help you study or work more effectively. This isn't a life-and-death decision. It's a dumb machine that will be out of date the moment you take it out of the box. Yet, you've got to make choices every step of the way. Do you want a Mac or a PC? Will a desktop or a notebook better suit your needs? How much hard drive space do you want? Do you want a Pentium processor or are you OK with a Celeron? What kind of software do you want? The list goes on. Sometimes the enormity of the choices available causes us to make no decision at all.

✓ *Our choices are too limited.* We look at all the options available, and none of them seem satisfactory. This problem seems to crop up in political elections. You look at the candidates and you don't like any of them. When you go to vote, you wish you could check a box that says, "None of the above" (or you just don't vote at all). Whether we're dealing with politics or churches, we stop short of making a decision because we aren't satisfied with the choices.

✓ *We experience inner conflict.* Arnold and Tompkins point out that the apostle Paul wrestled with this age-old problem when he wrote: "No matter which way I turn, I can't make myself do right. I want to, but I can't. When I want to do good, I don't. And when I try not to do wrong, I do it anyway" (Romans 7:18-19). If you are a Christian, you live with this kind of inner conflict more than most people. Your ability to make good decisions is clouded by what Arnold and Tompkins call "the influence of sinful desire."

Making Good Decisions One Step at a Time

We're going to stick with Arnold and Tompkins here, and not just because they run a company designed to teach people how to make good decisions. We like their simple, straightforward advice.

You see, many of us approach decision making as if we have to reinvent the wheel each time we make a decision. What a lot of work and worry! Yes, some decisions require new and original thinking, but most of the stuff we deal with on a daily basis can be handled by combining our experience with good old common sense.

Here's a seven-step commonsense approach that will be effective with 99 percent of the difficult decisions you face. To help illustrate and apply these steps, we're going to give you a hypothetical situation that requires a decision. (We suggest that you use one of your own, a decision you are facing right now. However, if you can't decide which one to use, feel free to stick with ours for the purpose of this exercise.)

- *Hypothetical situation*—You need to buy a new computer because your old one has just crashed, but you've been out of the computer market for a few years, so you're not sure which one to buy. (OK, you've been out of it for many years. Your old computer was an Atari.) You have budgeted between $1,500 and $2,000, and you have the money.
- *Your decision*—You need to choose one this week because you have an important project due.

Seven Steps to a Good Decision

We're going to lead you through this process by framing each step in the form of a question.

✓ **Why do I have to make a decision?**
This is obvious, but you need to take this step before proceeding. Is buying a new computer the only option to your current situation? Could you rent computer space at Kinko's? Could you use a friend's computer? Or do you have to have a computer of your own because you have to work at home (which is where you keep all of your snacks)?

✓ **What is it I am really trying to determine?**
After deciding that you really do need a computer this week, the big decision revolves around the brand, the power, the size, and the options available for the amount you want to spend. If it helps, write this stuff out on a sheet of paper (you can't type it in Word because your old computer is broken).

✓ **What do I want to achieve, preserve, or avoid?**
This is an important step, because it helps you narrow down your choices.

If you want to achieve speed, then you should choose the computer with the fastest processor available in your price range.

If you want to preserve compatibility with other computers, then a PC is better than a Mac. (We apologize to both of our readers who are Mac users.)

If you want to avoid the hassles of dealing with the customer service departments of those cheap catalog outfits, then you should buy from a local computer store.

✓ **What personal goals must be met by my decision?**
You have decided that your old desktop kept you confined to your office. You've heard that the new notebooks are just as powerful, so you'd like to go portable with this purchase, enabling you to be more "mobile" as you compute and word process stuff. This eliminates the desktop computer market and gets you to focus on the notebooks.

✓ **What alternatives meet the criteria I have set?**
Since there are so many brands available, you decide to purchase a computer magazine with an article comparing the different models that fit your standards. You narrow it down to three.

✓ **Which alternatives best fit my personal goals?**
This is where you actually go into the computer store, information in hand, ready to test the alternatives. You don't fear the pimply-faced teenage computer clerk because you have already narrowed down your options and you pretty much know what the experts are saying. You are basically looking at price, selection, and service.

✓ **What could go wrong?**

After determining the store's return policy, you decide the only thing that could go wrong is the hassle of bringing it back. The computer could always turn out to be a lemon, but the chances of that are remote. You decide to make your purchase, and you are delighted that the manufacturer has offered a rebate if you purchase by the end of the week. You know there are no guarantees in life, but you take your new computer home confident that you have made the right choice.

How to Make a No-Lose Decision

Dr. Susan Jeffers offers a shortcut to making good decisions in her book, *Feel the Fear and Do It Anyway*. If Arnold and Tompkins' seven steps are a little too complicated, try these five steps before making a decision:

1. **Focus on the positive aspects of your decision.**
2. **Do your homework.**
3. **Establish your priorities.**
4. **Trust your impulses.**
5. **Lighten up.**

The Art of Setting Goals

It's one thing to set some goals before purchasing a computer for the short term, and quite another to set goals that will improve your life and the lives of others in the long run.

Nobody knows goals better than the master motivator himself, Zig Ziglar. We found one of those "Dummies" books by Zig called *Success for Dummies*. According to Zig, if you want to be a success, you need to set goals. "It's one thing to want something to happen but quite another to actually set a goal to make it happen and work toward that goal in a conscious, dedicated manner," he writes.

Zig suggests that you set goals in six areas:

- *Spiritual*
- *Family*
- *Personal*
- *Physical*
- *Career*
- *Financial*

In each area, Zig advises that you set your goals based on five criteria. These are easy to remember, because they follow the acrostic SMART:

- Be *specific* about your goals.
- Make sure your goals are *measurable*.
- Your goals need to be *attainable* and *realistic*.
- Give your goals a *time* restriction.

Some of your goals should be quickly attainable, and others more long range. Many of your goals will be ones you want to repeat daily, such as exercise or reading the Bible. Others should be what one business executive we know calls "b-hags" (that stands for *big, hairy, audacious goals*). Remember, the biggest mistakes in life aren't necessarily the things you decided to do and did wrong. They are probably the things you decided not to try and never did.

Involving Others in Your Decisions

There are two ways to approach decision making. You can play it dumb and act like the Lone Ranger (who once said to his faithful sidekick Tonto: "If I want your opinion, I'll give it to you"). Or you can play it smart and seek the advice of others. Here's what the Book of Proverbs says:

People who despise advice will find themselves in trouble; those who respect it will succeed.

PROVERBS 13:13

That's pretty clear advice on getting advice, wouldn't you agree? And this doesn't just apply to individuals. Nations (and churches and companies and families) can benefit from the advice of others:

Without wise leadership, a nation falls; with many counselors, there is safety.

PROVERBS 11:14

Don't think you have to be the head of something in order to benefit from wise counsel. Anyone can—and should—have a whole team of advisors standing by just in case he or she needs input for a key decision. In our book *Real Life is a Contact Sport,* we talk about "designing your relationship network." The basic idea is to be intentional about the people you associate with, whether they are "situational acquaintances" (such as family, neighbors, and coworkers), or "intentional relationships" (such as friends, mentors, and your spouse, should you choose to marry).

Assemble a team of advisors from both categories. You don't have to have formal meetings or print up stationery, and you don't have to consult with each one on every decision, but it's always a good idea to involve someone else in your bigger decisions.

Here's our list of five categories of people who should be on your list of advisors. Next to each category, in the margin, write the name of the person who best fits the description we give you. If you can't think of anyone, make a decision to write in a name within the next thirty days.

Category	Description
Family	These are the people who know the "real you" (mainly because they gave birth to you, grew up with you, and put up with you). You may rely on a parent for advice, or even a kid brother. If you're married, trust your spouse to give you sound advice (it's always a good idea to ask before he or she feels compelled to tell you).

Category	Description
Friends	True friends want the best for you. You need two or three close friends who are available to help you or give you advice on a moment's notice. They should know that you would do the same for them.
Coworkers	Be careful of the "hot" stock tip at the coffee machine. On the other hand, someone who does the same stuff as you every day probably has some good advice from time to time.
Mentors	Choose your mentors carefully, meet with them regularly, and they will reward you with some of the best advice you will ever receive. In fact, that's what mentors are for. By the way, it's a great privilege to be asked to mentor someone else. Take your responsibility seriously.
Role Models	It's a good idea to have several role models in various areas of your life. You don't have to know them personally, but you should know about them. This comes from reading books about, or by, your role models, or perhaps talking to someone who does know them well. We suggest that you have role models that will feed your mind, body, and spirit.

Decision Making and the Will of God

A lot of people wrestle with the will of God, and it's no wonder. Since you can't touch, see, or hear God in a literal physical sense, how do you know when you are acting in his will? How do you know that God approves of the decisions you are making?

Without going into the very important and somewhat mysterious subject of God's will (we do that in our upcoming book, *Real Life to the Extreme*), we want to give you four very important principles about God's will and how it factors into your everyday decisions. These come from a classic book on the subject, *Decision Making and the Will of God* by Dr. Garry Friesen.

What Does the Bible Say?

If the Bible addresses your decision, then you should follow the Bible. This is what Dr. Friesen calls "God's moral will," which involves "the revealed commands in the Bible that teach how [we] ought to believe and live."

This may seem like a no-brainer, but if we were being completely honest with each other, we would admit that some of our difficult decisions are easily answered by a principle found in God's Word. For example, if you are struggling to decide whether or not you should move in with your girlfriend (or the other way around), then you either don't know what the Bible says about this particular subject, or you are choosing to disobey God. Obviously, one very important prerequisite to following this principle is that you must know what the Scriptures say. This doesn't mean you need to memorize the Bible, but you should study it thoroughly and systematically.

All Scripture is inspired by God and is useful to teach us what is true and to make us realize what is wrong with our lives. It straightens us out and teaches us to do what is right. It is God's way of preparing us in every way, fully equipped for every good thing God wants us to do.

2 TIMOTHY 3:16

Gather Input From Reliable Sources.

In those areas where the Bible gives no specific command or principle (Dr. Friesen calls these "nonmoral decisions"), we are free to use our own judgment, as long as our judgment is based on the wisdom of God's Word, the influence of the Holy Spirit, and the advice of spiritually minded people.

Will It Cause Someone to Stumble?

In all nonmoral decisions (areas not specifically addressed by Scripture), "the objective of the Christian is to make wise decisions on the basis of spiritual expediency." We take this to mean that your decisions should be based on your consideration for others before yourself. The apostle Paul talks about this with regard to doing certain things that may be perfectly acceptable for you, but may offend someone else (see 1 Corinthians 8:9-13).

Is It Something God Would Ask You to Do?

We need to see all of our decisions in the context of God's greater purposes for us (Dr. Friesen calls this "God's sovereign will"). This is a much more difficult concept to understand, let alone explain. Perhaps it is best expressed in one of our favorite verses in the Bible:

> *"For I know the plans I have for you," says the Lord. "They are plans for good and not for disaster, to give you a future and a hope. In those days when you pray, I will listen. If you look for me in earnest, I will be found by you," says the Lord.*
>
> JEREMIAH 29:11-13

We can't possibly see the wonderful things God has planned for us (see 1 Corinthians 2:9). We need to seek him through prayer and the reading of his Word. We need to trust God that he is working out his plans "for good and not for disaster" in our lives, little by little.

How to Recover From a Bad Decision

We titled this chapter "When Your Good Judgment Fails You" for a reason. It's going to happen, and you need to know what to do. Yet rather than dealing with ways to avoid bad decisions, we have attempted to share with you ways to make good decisions. Still, we need to address the reality of bad decisions, which happen when your good judgment fails you.

In truth, your good judgment never fails you. What happens is that you fail to exercise your good sense, or you act impulsively when you should have thought something through, or you deliberately go against what you know to be right. However it happens, it happens, usually after it's too late to change or fix, and a bad decision follows as surely as night follows the day, and you are left with the consequences. That's the bad news. The good news is that your good judgment is always there, waiting for you to use.

How do you recover from a bad decision? As we have done in every chapter, we want to bring our point home with a true story from the Bible. When it came to finding an example of someone in the Bible who made some bad decisions, the choice was easy. We chose King David, not because his choices were so bad (they were, but other Bible characters made equally bad decisions), but because he recovered from his bad decisions in a way the rest of us can emulate.

David's story is the stuff legends are made of. Like a swashbuckling character from the movies, David went from runt shepherd boy to giant killer to popular warrior to the king's enemy to king himself. From a human standpoint, David had it all: fame, fortune, family, and faith. From God's standpoint, David was a man after God's own heart. Yet despite the glories of his past, the security of his present, and the promise of his future, David chose to throw it all away with a series of bad decisions.

Our story opens with this descriptive and chilling account from the annals of Israel's history:

The following spring, the time of year when kings go to war, David sent Joab and the Israelite army to destroy the Ammonites. In the process they laid siege to the city of Rabbah. But David stayed behind in Jerusalem.

2 SAMUEL 11:1

David stayed behind. That was his first bad decision. He should have been with his army and his men. Then, in a perfect example of how one bad decision can lead to another and another, David seduced Bathsheba, the wife of one of his military officers who was off fighting in the war. Bathsheba became pregnant, and the king devised a plan to convince her husband, Uriah, that the child was his. David sent for Uriah and invited him to go home to see his wife. Being a loyal officer, Uriah refused, choosing instead to stay the night with the king's servants. Frustrated, David sent Uriah back to the front line, where he arranged for his loyal servant to be killed by the enemy.

Adultery, deceit, murder. David did it all through a series of bad decisions that came from a sinful heart. In a subtle yet profound way, the Bible says: "The Lord was very displeased with what David had done" (2 Samuel 11:27).

The Lord sent Nathan the prophet to confront David, who had not yet admitted his sin. When faced with his guilt, David confessed, "I have sinned against the Lord." These words then began his model recovery, which we have capsulated in a four-step process:

Step One: Confess Your Sins to the Lord.

Not all bad decisions are the result of sin, but many are. When confronted by your sin, either by someone else or your own telltale heart, confess it. God will forgive you (see 1 John 1:9). The alternative is to be "weak and miserable" (see Psalm 32:3).

Step Two: Be Prepared to Face the Consequences.

The first consequence David faced was the death of his baby (see 2 Samuel 12:14). And from that point forward he struggled to maintain control of his kingdom. "Remember that you can't ignore God and get away with it. You will always reap what you sow" (Galatians 6:7-8).

Step Three: Realize That God Gives You Grace.

Chuck Swindoll writes: "Grace means that God, in forgiving you, gives you the strength to endure the consequences."

Step Four: Learn From Your Mistakes.

With God's help, don't make the same bad decisions again. Recognize that good decisions come from a "clean heart" and a "right spirit" (Psalm 51:10).

Another Side of Failure

Over the last few chapters we have been dealing with failure as it relates to the stuff at which people usually fail—relationships, love, work, finances, and decisions. Now we're going to turn to something you don't normally put in the same category as failure, and that's faith.

People don't think of faith as something at which you fail. Either you have faith or you don't. At least that's what you've always thought, right? Well, there may be more to it than that. As you will see in the next chapter, faith isn't as simple as it seems, at least not when you look below the surface. Faith is like a muscle: it grows when you exercise it and shrinks when you ignore it. If you want a strong faith that succeeds, read on.

> We trust not because "a god" exists,
> but because this God exists.

—C.S. Lewis

CHAPTER 9

When Your Faith Seems Futile

Have you ever done something that required you to have faith in someone else? We're not talking about loaning your friend five bucks, and then having faith that he will pay you back. The kind of faith we mean is real life-and-death faith, the kind that requires you to literally place your life into the hands of another. Allow us to illustrate.

Legend has it that Karl Wallenda (gee, we're sure talking about him a lot in this book) was about to walk the high wire in front of a large crowd. Before he performed his death-defying feat, he turned to the crowd and asked, "Do you believe I can do this?"

"Yes, we believe!" the crowd answered.

Wallenda said it again. "Do you believe?"

"Yes!" the crowd answered again, this time with more enthusiasm.

"If you believe, then who among you will step forward and sit on my shoulders as I walk the high wire?"

This time there was no answer. The crowd was as silent as a stone. When no one stepped forward, Wallenda turned away from the crowd and walked the high wire—alone.

Did the crowd believe? Of course. They believed that Karl Wallenda could walk the high wire. But did they have *faith* in Karl Wallenda? No. They *believed* he could do what he had done a thousand times before, but no one truly *trusted* Karl Wallenda (trust is the essence of faith). No one was willing to fully commit by putting his or her life on the line. (By the way, this wasn't the time he fell.)

Everyday Faith

We're not sure if this story is true or just another urban legend, but the moral of the story comes through loud and clear. It's one thing to believe, and quite another to have faith. Let's go back to our opening question for a minute. *Have you ever done something that required you to have faith in another person?* Only this time, think about Karl Wallenda and life and death. So what's your answer?

Well, unless you sit at home all day and never get out, you most certainly do have faith in other people—every single day of your life. Whenever you leave your house or apartment and get behind the wheel of that two-ton metal contraption you use to transport yourself from one place to another, you have faith that some other driver out there isn't going to careen to your side of the road and hit you head-on. More than believing that it's safe to drive, you have faith as well, because you literally put your life into the hands of other people (and may we add, they put their lives into your hands).

How about doctors? Do you have faith in medical professionals? We have a friend who was diagnosed with cancer. As these things often go, it all happened very fast. The doctors found evidence of cancer and immediately prescribed an aggressive treatment involving chemotherapy. Our friend was understandably shaken and a bit bewildered by the swift course of action. This was his life they were dealing with. Had he merely believed in the doctors, but not had faith in their judgment, he would not have allowed them to pump devastating chemicals into his body. But he did have faith. He put his life into their hands, even though he didn't know what the outcome would be.

You see, every one of us exercises faith in something or someone every day. Sometimes the exercise is so routine that you don't even think about it, like driving a car or eating at Denny's. Other times you are very aware of committing your life to another, and it's all you can think about. It's as if you're in that crowd and you're telling Karl Wallenda, "I'll climb on your shoulders and walk the high wire with you!"

Faith and God

Now, let's think about faith in the traditional sense most of us think about when we hear the word "faith," as in "Christian faith" or "faith in God." What comes to your mind? If you were to list some of your ideas about faith as they relate to God, what would they be? Here are some we came up with:

- Having a belief system
- Believing that God exists
- Feeling that God loves us
- Knowing that we're going to heaven
- Trusting in Jesus
- Being willing to put our lives on the line for our faith

We listed only six ideas about faith, and to be perfectly honest, we're not really sure about that last one. We'd like to say that we would die for our faith, but if push came to shove, would we really be willing to die for our faith?

And what about those times when we seem to have more doubt than faith? What about those who believe that faith itself is more important than the object of faith? In other words, it doesn't matter what you believe, as long as you believe (oh, and it helps to be sincere). Suddenly this faith thing isn't so cut-and-dry, is it? No wonder people struggle with the idea of having faith.

When you really think about this stuff (and we hope you are), you can't help but wonder about something else. Do people struggle with their faith, or are they in fact struggling with God? You may not agree with us, but we think the reason why people have so many different concepts of faith is that they have so many concepts of God—most of them wrong. Patrick Morley once wrote:

> *"There is the God who is, and there is the God we want, and they are not the same God."*

If you define God by what people want, then you're going to get a lot of different ideas about God:

- He's the God who gives you what you want (this is the *Santa Claus* God).
- He's the God who won't send you to hell (this is the *Pollyanna* God).
- He's the God of fire and brimstone (this is the *TV Evangelist* God).
- He's the kindly grandfather God (this is the *George Burns* God).
- He's the God of your inner spirit (this is the *Oprah* God).
- He's God your little buddy (this is the *Gilligan* God).

If your faith seems futile at times, maybe you are putting too much emphasis on your faith and not enough on God. Do you feel like a failure in your Christian life? Perhaps your concept of God is not what it should be.

Faith in Faith

Did you know that it's possible to have faith in faith rather than faith in God? It's not just possible, but it has become quite the rage in our culture.

There's no question that Americans are a religious bunch. But a recent study conducted by Public Agenda found that three-quarters of religious Americans think it doesn't matter which religion you believe in, as long as you believe in something. More than half of all religious people say it's not necessary to believe in God to have good values. In other words, people have faith in faith.

It's OK to wonder about your faith and to be confused about God. This is pretty big stuff. Faith and God aren't subjects you study for a few months in Sunday school or a religion class and then go, "Well, I've got it!" Understanding what your faith is all about isn't like mastering the art of tying your shoe.

Likewise, knowing God isn't like learning to ride a bike. These are complicated, difficult, and mysterious issues. But that doesn't let you off the hook! Faith and God may not be easy, but they are awfully important (important things are never easy, by the way). In fact, they are life-and-death important.

But wait! Don't get discouraged. We're not here to scare you off. If you feel like a spiritual failure, we don't want to leave you with a futile feeling. The Christian faith may be a complicated, difficult, mysterious process, but it's easy to get started.

Your Faith Is a Puzzle

Picture in your mind one of those thousand-piece jigsaw puzzles. You don't just dump out the pieces on a table only to throw up your hands in frustration because you can't finish it in five minutes. You understand that the process of putting the puzzle together is going to take a while.

So what do you do first? You start with one piece—usually a corner—and you build your puzzle one piece at a time. You look for patterns in the pieces. You watch for matching colors and images. Most of all, you look at the finished picture on the front of the box for your ultimate reference point. The picture is the objective. It's why you're putting this puzzle together in the first place. Without the picture, well, then you are lost, and there's really no point to the process. If you don't know what the end result looks like, you can begin but you'll never finish.

Your faith is like that puzzle. There are a thousand pieces that bring up a thousand questions. If you try to put it together without an objective or a point of reference, you are going to be constantly frustrated. In fact, you'll probably quit altogether. You need that final picture even before you begin your faith journey. And just what is the picture on the box of faith? Here's a hint: it has something to do with God. But since God is a Spirit (see John 4:24) and no one has seen God, the picture must be of something closely related to God. Let's find out as we explore the pieces of the faith puzzle.

Faith Puzzle Piece #1 – Knowledge

In order for faith to begin, you must begin with knowing God. Here's what the apostle Paul wrote to the Roman church:

> *But how can they call on him to save them unless they believe in him? And how can they believe in him if they have never heard about him? And how can they hear about him unless someone tells them?*
>
> ROMANS 10:14

Somewhere along the line, someone told you about God. Most likely you were a little kid, and even if you didn't understand a whole lot, the concept of God stuck with you. Truth is, everybody thinks about God sometime (even the atheist thinks about God) because God himself built this knowledge into our hearts (see Romans 1:19). But just because you think about God doesn't mean you believe he exists. That's another level of knowledge that comes from investigating the evidence.

Knowledge of God's Existence
In our book *Bruce & Stan's Guide to God*, we list the four classic arguments for the existence of God, which go something like this:

- The very fact that all people think about God points to his existence (see Romans 1:19). This is called the *ontological* argument.
- Every cause in the universe has an effect, and ultimately there has to be an original First Cause. There is no better explanation of the First Cause than God (see Hebrews 3:4). This is called the *cosmological* argument.
- The incredible design and order of the universe points to an intelligent designer, not random chance. Only God fits the bill (see Psalm 19:1; Romans 1:20). This is called the *teleological* argument.

- Every human being has a built-in sense of right and wrong, also known as a moral code, designed in our DNA by our Creator (see Romans 2:15). This is called the *moral* argument.

Knowledge of God's Person

Believing that God exists is like knowing that Julia Roberts exists. He's a persona, not a person. You don't really know God. Knowing God means knowing something about his personality. The best place to find out is in the Bible, which is where we came up with these fascinating personality traits:

- *God is eternal.* He always was and he always will be. There was never a time when God did not exist (see Psalm 90:2).
- *God is holy.* He is absolutely perfect (the Bible word is righteous). His moral character has no flaw (see Isaiah 6:3).
- *God is just.* He is completely fair and impartial (see Deuteronomy 32:4).
- *God doesn't change.* He is the same always, and he cannot be changed (see Malachi 3:6).
- *God is omnipotent.* He is all-powerful. There's nothing God can't do, except those things that go against his holy nature (see Revelation 19:6).
- *God is omniscient.* He knows everything past, present, and future. And he knows you completely (see Psalm 139:1-4).
- *God is love.* God's justice and holiness require that he hold us accountable for our rebellion to him (that's what sin is). But his love caused him to send his Son, Jesus, as a sacrifice for our sins (see 1 John 4:9-10).

Knowledge of God's Plan

OK, so you know God exists, you know a little about his personality. That's nice. Do you know his plan? Well, you need to, because this is the life-and-death part of faith and God. Here is God's plan as summarized in the best-known verse in the Bible, John 3:16—

- *"For God so loved the world ..."* Every one of us is a sinner. All of us fall far short of God's perfect standard (see Romans 3:23). Without God's intervention of love, we would die in our sins (Romans 6:23).
- *"... that he gave his only Son ..."* God didn't wait until we met his

standard to save us (mainly because we can never do that on our own). He sent Jesus into the world while we were sinners in order to pay the price for our sin (see Romans 5:8).

- "...*so that everyone who believes in him...*" Nobody is excluded from God's plan of salvation. Anyone who calls on the name of Jesus will be saved (see Acts 4:12).

- "...*will not perish but have eternal life.*" God's plan has always centered on Jesus Christ, and it has always included bringing us back into a relationship with him forever (see Ephesians 1:5).

Faith Puzzle Piece #2 – Agreement

We're going to say something here that's pretty important (OK, so we say a lot of stuff that's important, but this is *really* important). *Knowledge alone won't save you.* You can know God exists. You can know about God. You can even know the details of God's plan. But if that's as far as you go, you could still be separated from God for eternity. The Bible says, "...even the demons believe this" (James 2:19). Last time we checked, the demons have no shot at eternity with God in heaven.

Knowledge isn't enough. There's another piece of the faith puzzle that is absolutely essential. You have to *agree* with God's plan, which centers on Jesus and Jesus alone. This is where a lot of people get hung up in the whole faith process. "How can anyone be so arrogant as to believe that there's only one way to God?" they ask indignantly. We have just one answer: *He's God and you're not.* Call it what you want, God's plan is very specific, and no one knew it better than Jesus:

I am the way, the truth, and the life. No one can come to the Father except through me.

JOHN 14:6

This is God's plan. He has designed the agreement that stands between us and salvation. More correctly, this agreement makes our salvation possible.

Salvation Is Such an Old-Fashioned Word

The word *salvation* isn't exactly a politically correct word these days, mainly because if you need to be saved, it means you're in danger of losing your life, and who wants to think about that?

Besides, if you happen to believe that all dogs—er, people—go to heaven, then who needs to be saved? Think of it this way. If you saw a man drowning in a lake, you would do everything you could to save him. You wouldn't tell him, "Oh, you're not in any danger. If you just believe that you won't drown, you'll be fine. Besides, I don't think you're really drowning." No, you would send out a lifeboat, or you would jump in and try to save him yourself.

That's what God has done for us. He knows we're drowning, even if we don't. He has already jumped in the lake in the person of Jesus Christ, who is the ultimate lifeboat. Old-fashioned or not, salvation is what we need.

Faith Puzzle Piece #3 – Decision

Remember that last very important thing we said? (It's on the previous page.) Here's another very important thing. It's not enough just to agree that God's plan through Jesus Christ is the only way to be saved. You have to decide to depend on Jesus for your salvation.

When you decide to accept Jesus as your personal Savior, your faith moves from objective to saving faith. Here's how Wayne Grudem defines *saving faith:* "Saving faith is trust in Jesus Christ as a living person for forgiveness of sins and for eternal life with God." This is where you move beyond belief in the facts to a personal trust in Jesus to save you.

Now we're getting to the root of faith. This is the Karl Wallenda kind of faith we talked about at the beginning of the chapter. This is where you truly trust God to wipe out your sin debt (and with it the consequence of eternal death) and give you eternal life through Jesus (see Romans 6:23). Why trust God? Because God—and only God—is completely trustworthy.

God is not a man, that he should lie. He is not a human, that he should change his mind. Has he ever spoken and failed to act? Has he ever promised and not carried it through?

NUMBERS 23:19

When you find someone this trustworthy (especially when it's your life we're talking about here), you grab onto him. You don't just believe in God; you don't just agree with God; you make a decision to follow God fully.

Without wavering, let us hold tightly to the hope we say we have, for God can be trusted to keep his promise.

HEBREWS 10:23

Three More Faith Puzzle Pieces

Repentance

Faith is like a coin: It has two sides. On one side (call it heads) is the trust part of faith in which you move toward God. But in order to move toward God and your new life in Christ, you have to move away from your old life of sin. This is called repentance, and it is the flip side of the coin (it's also a faith puzzle piece). The apostle Paul said it this way:

I have had one message for Jews and Gentiles—the necessity of turning from sin and turning to God, and of faith in our Lord Jesus.

ACTS 20:21

Salvation is "once and for all," but the process of repentence and faith continue throughout your life. In other words, you don't need to keep asking God to save you. As Grudem writes, "*initial* saving faith and *initial* repentance occur only once in our lives, and when they occur they constitute true conversion." But turning from sin must continue because you still have the capacity to sin. You need to continue to have faith in Christ to help you live your Christian life.

Assurance

Here's the question we get asked more than any other: "Can I ever lose my salvation?" That's a great question, and if you don't know the answer, it can be very troubling.

Part of the reason this question comes up is that you're not always going to "feel" saved. That's why you can never rely on your feelings. R.C. Sproul writes: "Although a true Christian cannot lose his salvation, he can lose his assurance of salvation." So how do you get your assurance back? By continuing to turn from your sins as you turn to Christ in obedience to him.

Do you feel as if God isn't even listening to you? David wrote in the Psalms: "If I had not confessed the sin in my heart, my Lord would not have listened" (Psalm 66:18). In our view, prayer is a pretty big part of assurance, but God will hear you only if you have asked him to forgive you for choosing to sin instead of choosing to obey him (see 1 John 1:9).

Besides prayer, you need to read the Bible. Nothing will bring assurance to your heart better than a daily dose of God's Word. Here's where you'll find comforting verses like this one from Jesus himself:

My sheep recognize my voice; I know them and they follow me. I give them eternal life, and they will never perish.

JOHN 10:27-28

Works

The final faith puzzle piece we're going to talk about is works, or what the Bible calls "good deeds," as in "faith that does not result in good deeds is useless" (James 2:20). It's true that works are a critical part of the saving faith process, but your good works can never save you. This is made clear in several places in the Bible, especially in Paul's letter to the church at Ephesus:

God saved you by his special favor when you believed. And you can't take credit for this; it is a gift from God. Salvation is not a reward for the good things we have done, so none of us can boast about it.

EPHESIANS 2:8-9

If our salvation depended on our performance, then none of us would make it, because none of us can score a perfect "10" before God in the Olympics of life, and that's what he requires. Jesus scored the perfect "10" on our behalf, which is God's free gift to us. However, God doesn't save us just so we can sit around doing nothing, as if we were waiting for our "wings." The next verse in Ephesians pretty well sums it up:

> *For we are God's masterpiece. He has created us anew in Christ Jesus, so that we can do the good things he planned for us long ago.*
>
> EPHESIANS 2:10

God wants us to do "good things," not in our own strength, but in Christ's strength. "For I can do everything with the help of Christ who gives me the strength I need," writes Paul (Philippians 4:13). Your works must be the natural outgrowth of your faith. That's what James means when he writes, "Faith that doesn't show itself by good deeds is no faith at all—it is dead and useless" (James 2:17).

Are You Getting the Picture?

Earlier in this section we talked about the cover on the box of the faith puzzle. Have you guessed what's on the cover? More correctly, have you guessed *who* is on the cover?

The answer is Jesus, who is "the visible image of the invisible God" (Colossians 1:15). He is the one "on whom our faith depends from start to finish" (Hebrews 12:2). Without the life, death, and resurrection of Jesus, our faith would be pointless. In fact, our lives would be pointless, because Jesus "holds all creation together" (Colossians 1:17). As you live your Christian life, keep your eyes and your faith on Jesus (see Hebrews 12:2).

Faith and Doubt

Philip Yancey has written a profound book called *Reaching for the Invisible God*. In it he writes that people of faith will naturally doubt. This doesn't mean that you live in a constant state of wondering if this whole Christian life is merely a contrivance to make us all feel better. What it means is that at one time or another, every one of us has said (or at least thought), "What if God really isn't out there?" Don't worry. You aren't losing your salvation. God isn't standing by in heaven ready to slap you upside the head if you express feelings of doubt. It's part of your faith.

"When I wish to explore how faith works, I usually sneak in by the back door of doubt," Yancy writes, "for I best learn about my own need for faith during its absence. God's invisibility guarantees I will experience times of doubt." Yancey points out that by its very nature faith must make room for doubt. If we were 100 percent sure of things, why would we need faith?

Doubt is the skeleton in the closet of faith.

—Philip Yancey

The truth is that God has deliberately shielded himself from us in certain ways. (That's a good thing. If God revealed everything about himself, we couldn't handle it. We are, after all, mere mortals.) Much about God remains a mystery. That's why faith is such an important part of the process of knowing God. Faith combines the knowledge of a God who has proven himself to be faithful in the world and in your life. You can read about God's great faithfulness in the Bible (see Lamentations 3:23). But the greatest reward for your faith will be your own personal experience as you trust God every day.

God has been faithful in the past, he is faithful to you right now, and he promises to be faithful in the future.

What is faith? It is the confident assurance that what we hope for is going to happen. It is the evidence of things we cannot yet see.

HEBREWS 11:1

Successful Faith

There is no better model for a successful life of faith than the apostle Paul. He was brought up to be very religious, and he trained under the greatest religious teachers of his day. But he didn't have saving faith. In fact, Paul was one of the chief persecutors of Christians in the early church (see Acts 9: 1-2). Then Paul met the Lord on the road to Damascus, and his life was transformed. He became the greatest missionary the world has ever known, and he ended up writing much of the New Testament.

Paul had an amazing faith, but he also had his struggles. He struggled with sin (see Romans 7:18-20). He struggled against persecution, pain, and danger (see 2 Corinthians 11:23-27). He struggled with the inconsistent behavior of the churches he worked so hard to help (see 2 Corinthians 12:19-21). Yet through it all Paul's faith caused him to be thankful (see Philippians 1:3), confident (see Philippians 4:13), positive (see Romans 8:31), enthusiastic (see Romans 8:38-39), and content (see Philippians 4:11).

What was the secret of Paul's success? He took one faith step at a time.

I don't mean to say that I have already achieved these things or that I have already reached perfection! But I keep working toward that day when I will finally be all that Christ Jesus saved me for and wants me to be. No, dear brothers and sisters, I am still not all I should be, but I am focusing all my energies on this one thing: Forgetting the past and looking forward to what lies ahead, I strain to reach the end of the race and receive the prize for which God, through Christ Jesus, is calling us up to heaven.

PHILIPPIANS 3:12-14

A life of faith is not futile. It is the most satisfying, exciting, and rewarding life there is. It's the kind of life that will someday cause you to say:

I have fought a good fight, I have finished the race, and I have remained faithful.

2 TIMOTHY 4:7

PART THREE

Rising Above Failure

The chief factor in any man's success or failure must be his own character.

—Theodore Roosevelt

In the last few chapters we have examined how the failures of your circumstances can be changed into successes. Now it is time to shift the examination from your circumstances to your character.

The depth of a person's character is revealed by the manner in which he or she responds to failure and success. Failure tempts a person to despair. Success invites pride. The character of an individual will determine whether failure can be faced with dignity and success can be displayed with humility.

In the concluding chapters we ignore the external *circumstances* and talk about internal *character*. We'll discuss how past failure in moral or ethical issues is not proof of a defect in character but that character is revealed by the response to such failings. We'll also talk about the maturity that is necessary to forgive one's failures in order to enjoy future success.

Through much of this book we have been talking about failure and success in terms of what you do. Now we will be looking at failure and success from the perspective of who you are. We think you'll find it to be an interesting viewpoint. It is not often that you get the opportunity to see yourself from the inside out.

> The ultimate measure of a man is not where he stands
> in moments of comfort and convenience, but where
> he stands at times of challenge and controversy.

—Martin Luther King

CHAPTER 10

Learning From Failure

A scorpion, being a poor swimmer, asked a turtle to carry him on his back across a river.

"Are you mad?" exclaimed the turtle. "You'll sting me while I'm swimming and I'll drown."

"My dear turtle," laughed the scorpion, "if I were to sting you, you would drown and I would go down with you. Now where is the logic in that?"

"You're right," cried the turtle. "Hop on!"

The scorpion climbed aboard and halfway across the river gave the turtle a mighty sting. As they both sank to the bottom, the turtle resignedly said, "Do you mind if I ask you something? You said there'd be no logic in your stinging me. Why did you do it?"

"It has nothing to do with logic," the drowning scorpion sadly replied. "It's just my character."

* * * * * * *

Your character is the ultimate reflection of who you are. Like the scorpion, it doesn't really matter what you say. Your character is revealed by what you do.

Character is what you do when nobody is looking.

—Henry Huffman

Huffman's definition suggests that a person's true character is revealed only in private when that person is free to act however he or she wants, unrestrained by the influence of others.

The famous golfer Bobby Jones illustrated Huffman's definition of character. Jones was playing in a national championship golf match. He drove his ball into the woods and walked unaccompanied into the trees to take his next shot. (This was before the advent of roving television cameras that track each shot more closely than NASA monitors its spacecraft.)

After taking his shot and walking out of the woods, Jones penalized himself one extra stroke because, unseen to anyone else, he accidentally nudged his golf ball. That one-stroke penalty was the margin of his defeat. If he hadn't admitted to the penalty stroke, he would have been in a tie for first place and possibly would have won the championship in the playoff round. No one would have known ... except himself.

Huffman's definition and Jones' story reveal an interesting aspect about character:

> **A person with character does the right thing regardless of the consequences.**

If you have character, then your behavior is determined by your sense of right and wrong. The propriety of your conduct is all that matters. You don't have to be concerned with collateral issues such as:

- Is your response going to be popular?
- Are some people going to criticize what you have done?

- Will you come out of this situation looking good?
- Are your personal interests being advanced?

> **Character is all about doing the right thing simply because that is the right thing to do.**

There is another interesting aspect about character:

> **A person of character does the right thing even in the minor, insignificant details of life.**

Most people do the right thing when a major issue is involved that has serious consequences:

- You don't steal money from the Brink's truck as you walk by;
- As much as you would like a new car, you return it to the showroom instead of to your own garage when you have concluded your test-drive; and
- As easy as it might be to do with a strategic transformation of a decimal point into a comma and the addition of a few extra zeroes, you refrain from altering the numbers on that $1.00 rebate into a check for $1,000.00.

Most people also do the right thing when the circumstances make the appropriate behavior painfully obvious:

- You slow down to the speed limit when a highway patrol officer comes up behind you on the freeway;
- You don't peek through that little curtain on the airliner that separates you from the ritzy passengers in first class; and
- You don't cool off on a sweltering summer day by standing naked in the frozen food aisle at the grocery store.

But it is often harder to display character when you are dealing with the minor, seemingly insignificant details of life:

- When you leave the drive-thru window at Pork-on-a-Stick, do you return after you discover that the server gave you thirty-seven cents too much in change?
- When you are submitting a voucher to your employer to be reimbursed for your business trip, do you "round up" the total by a few miles?
- When you are claiming a deduction on your income taxes for that bag of used underwear that you gave to the Salvation Army, do you exaggerate the value of your worn and tattered undies?
- If the movie theatre prohibits bringing food and beverages into the building, do you try to sneak them in under your coat?

The amount of money involved in each of these examples is just a pittance. Most people wouldn't think that these issues are of any ethical significance. But they matter to a person of character.

This chapter is all about character, but we aren't going to spend much more time talking about the positive side of it. We want to focus on what it means when you don't do the right thing. Does that mean you are completely void of character? Are you a moral and ethical failure if you give in to social pressure or the temptation for self-preservation?

If you are disappointed in yourself because your behavior has evidenced a lack of character, you should be encouraged. The fact that you feel bad about it shows that you have character. Maybe you aren't as bad off as you think. Maybe you just need a little help in determining the appropriate response, instead of relying on your gut reaction.

A Guy Who Really Blew It Big Time

It is personally discouraging when you do the wrong thing in private and are confronted with your own lack of integrity and character. But it is even worse when you have a lapse of character in public and everyone knows about it. So try to imagine how devastating it would be to have your character flaw recorded in a best-selling book that people would be reading for centuries. That is exactly what happened to the apostle Peter.

It was the night before Jesus was going to be crucified. Jesus was having one last dinner with his disciples. He didn't come right out and say that he was going to be killed, but he did explain to his disciples that he wasn't going to be around much longer. Then Peter asked a pertinent question (and here we'll pick up the dialogue exactly as it is recorded in John 13:36-38):

> "Lord, where are you going?"
>
> And Jesus replied, "You can't go with me now, but you will follow me later."
>
> "But why can't I come now, Lord?" he asked. "I am ready to die for you."
>
> Jesus answered, "Die for me? No, before the rooster crows tomorrow morning, you will deny three time that you even know me."

At that point Peter couldn't imagine that he would ever deny knowing Jesus. But he also couldn't imagine the events that would follow in the next few hours. Before long, Jesus had been arrested and was being hauled back and forth by the soldiers in the middle of the night between several phony trials. As Peter was standing around in the courtyard waiting to hear the verdict, a woman approached him. According to John 18:17-18 and 25-27, Peter folded under the pressure and ended the night with the three pitiful denials Jesus had predicted:

> The woman asked Peter, "Aren't you one of Jesus' disciples?"
>
> "No," he said, "I am not."
>
> The guards and the household servants were standing around a charcoal fire they had made because it was cold. And Peter stood there with them, warming himself. Meanwhile, as Peter was standing by the fire, they asked him again, "Aren't you one of his disciples?"
>
> "I am not," he said.
>
> But one of the household servants of the high priest, a relative of the man whose ear Peter had cut off, asked, "Didn't I see you out there in the olive grove with Jesus?" Again Peter denied it. And immediately a rooster crowed.

Maybe it wouldn't have been so bad if Peter hadn't boasted of his loyalty to Jesus. But he had. Maybe it wouldn't have been so bad if Peter had only denied his friendship with Jesus once. But he did it three times.

We aren't critical of Peter for denying Jesus. How could we be critical of him when we have denied Jesus in our own ways each time that we have failed to talk about him because we thought it would be awkward or we felt self-conscious about it? Actually, we can sympathize a bit with Peter. We are sure that he felt miserable and useless. In other words, he felt like a failure because he showed a complete lack of character.

Isn't it great that the Bible's story of Peter doesn't stop with the cock-a-doodle-do? In John 21:15-22, we have the chance to read that Jesus didn't consider Peter as useless. In fact, Jesus asked Peter three times, "Do you love me?" Peter answered three times in the affirmative. (We don't think it is a mere coincidence that the number of times he said, "You know that I love you" is the exact number of times that he denied Christ.) This interchange between them allowed Peter to examine his true feelings and commitment to Jesus, and it also allowed Jesus to confirm that Peter had a role in God's plan.

When You Blow It Big Time

We don't know the circumstances of your character failings, but we don't imagine that yours can match the severity of what Peter did. And if Peter was still useful to God after denying Christ, there is no reason why you should assume that your character failings are fatal.

Peter's life story shows that his character chart hit its lowest dip on that fateful night in the courtyard. On that night, he revealed a lack of character, but from that point on the conduct of his life showed that he was a man of character. He didn't lead a perfect life after that (Paul confronted him on one occasion over an issue of hypocrisy), but he never again displayed the failings of that night in the courtyard.

Your character failings, whatever they have been, can be the low point on your character chart. There is no reason why the degree of your character has to be a flat line along the bottom of the chart. It can head in an upward direction from this day forward. Peter recovered from his character failings, and so can you.

How Can You Determine "The Right Thing" To Do?

If you are sincere about wanting to recover from your character failings of the past and to start charting your character in an upward direction (and we believe you are), then you are going to be intent on doing the right thing in every situation. Much of the time that will be easy. Deciding what is the right thing to do is a no-brainer when:

- Someone asks you to lie to cover for them at work;
- You've messed up at work and are tempted to lie to cover for yourself; or
- You pick up your car at the service center, you notice that they forgot to charge you for the oil change.

But there are other times and other situations when it isn't so easy to determine the correct behavior. Sometimes there doesn't appear to be a clear distinction between black and white; the entire circumstance seems gray. In these situations you can see reasons for different behavior, and they all make some sense. These situations present you with ethical dilemmas for which the solution is not readily identifiable.

The term "ethical dilemma" was around long before it was made popular by "Dr. Laura" on her radio and television show. We even hesitate to use the term for fear that you might think that we are talking about the kind of situation that is presented by her typical caller. For those of you who have never heard her show, allow us to give you a fictionalized example of the type of "ethical dilemma" that a caller might have presented to her:

Dr. Laura, I'm married but presently separated from my spouse and living with another lover. Lately that attraction has started to wear off. I still like this other person, but I don't know if I want to keep living with this other person if it is possible that I might be more attracted to someone else later.

My mother is disgusted with my behavior and says that I can't come to my father's birthday dinner if I insist on bringing my live-in lover. Here's my ethical dilemma: "Should I buy him a birthday present or just send a card?"

We suspect that your ethical dilemmas are going to occur in a context that is a little more related to real life. Perhaps your situation will involve discovering that a fellow employee is cheating on his time sheets at work. You are torn between your friendship with the other employee and your duty of loyalty to your company. You don't want to do anything that would get your friend fired because you know his family needs the income, but you also don't want the clients of your firm being unfairly overbilled. You want to do the right thing, but you don't know whether that means:

- Confronting your coworker and attempting to persuade him to confess his dishonesty to the supervisor;
- Telling your coworker to stop cheating from this point forward or you will be obligated to report him to the supervisor;
- Skipping the personal confrontation and going directly to the supervisor with what you know; or
- Leaving an anonymous note in the suggestion box that the company needs to institute security measures to curb the use of fraudulent time sheets.

Sometimes the correct response to an ethical dilemma is dictated by a professional code of conduct:

- Lawyers' and physicians' professional conduct is guided by standards adopted by their respective professional associations.
- Religious and counseling professionals adhere to strict guidelines concerning client confidentiality, with permitted exceptions if the client presents a potential harm to self or others.
- Organizations like fraternities and sororities have rituals that serve as statements of organizational standards and values.
- Some institutions adopt an honor code.

The cadet will not lie, cheat or steal, nor tolerate those who do.

—Code of Honor, U.S. Military Academy,
West Point, NY

But most of the time you won't have a code of conduct to guide you in making the right decision. You'll have to use your judgment. And maybe that's why you worry, because your judgment in the past has been a little faulty. Maybe you are worried that your personal judgment is too susceptible to your own subjective feelings. You don't want to make a decision based on your gut reaction and then realize that you blew it when you hear the rooster crow.

Many scholars in the fields of personal development and psychology have developed systems for ethical decision making. Some are more easily understood than others. Here is a brief overview of three such models for ethical problem solving:

#1: The Rest Four-Component Decision-Making Model

In his treatise, "Moral Development in Young Adults," James Rest developed what he considered to be a practical decision-making model based on moral reasoning and an ethic of care.

According to Rest, moral development or moral behavior is composed not of a single process, but of four distinct yet interrelated functions. The Rest four-component decision-making model looks like this:

Component I: Moral Sensitivity (interpreting a situation as moral)
- a. Being aware of the situation's moral dimension (i.e., that the welfare of another person is at stake)
- b. Recognizing how possible courses of action affect all parties involved

Component II: Moral Judgment (defining the moral ideal course of action)
- c. Determining what should be done
- d. Formulating a plan of action that applies as moral standard or ideal (for example, justice)

Component III: Moral Motivation (deciding what to do)
- e. Evaluating the various courses of action for how they would serve moral or nonmoral values (for example, political sensitivity, professional aspirations)
- f. Deciding what to do

Component IV: Moral Action (executing and implementing a moral plan of action)

  g. Acting as one intended to act; following through with that decision

  h. Assisted by perseverance, resoluteness, strong character, core values, the strength of one's convictions, and so on

For us, Rest's model for decision making is not practical. We can't use it because we get a headache just reading it and trying to figure out what it means. It is just not workable for making on-the-spot decisions (because we'd have to carry his book with us to remember all of the component parts).

#2: The Ethical Principles of Aristotle
Several scholars have tweaked ethical principles that were articulated by Aristotle. Karen Strohm Kitchener, a professor of education, adapted five principles for use as means of moral reasoning and ethical decision making. In deciding what is "the right thing" to do, these five principles are supposed to give you guidance in making your decision:

1. *Respecting autonomy:* Your decision should recognize that other individuals should be allowed the freedom to develop their values and that they have the right to act independently.
2. *Doing no harm:* Your decision should not be harmful, either psychologically or physically, to others.
3. *Benefiting others:* Your decision should promote the interests of your organization or of others above your personal interests and self-gain.
4. *Being just:* Your decision should treat people fairly and equally.
5. *Being faithful:* Your decision should be consistent with promises you have previously made and should be premised on relationships and trust.

These principles may be helpful in determining a correct course of action by focusing on how your decisions will affect others.

#3: The Twelve-Question Checklist

Checklists are easier for many people, and an ethical-decision list of questions was developed by L.L. Nash and published in *Training & Development Magazine*. As with the five ethical principles, these twelve questions are to be used before you commit to an action or a decision.

1. Have you defined the problem accurately?
2. How would you define the problem if you stood on the other side of the fence?
3. How did this situation occur in the first place?
4. To whom and to what do you give your loyalty as a person and as a member of the organization?
5. What is your intention in making this decision?
6. How does this intention compare with the probable results?
7. Whom could your decision or action injure?
8. Can you discuss the problem with the affected parties before you make your decision?
9. Are you confident that your position will be as valid over a long period of time as it seems now?
10. Could you disclose without qualms your decision or action to your boss, the president of the board of directors, your family, society as a whole?
11. What is the symbolic potential of your action if understood? What if it is misunderstood?
12. Under what conditions would you allow exceptions to your stand?

Of the three methods, we like these twelve questions the best. For us, they are the easiest to think through. There is just one problem. We can't remember all of them. Oh sure, we can look them up in our files, but that doesn't help us if we are making an on-the-spot decision. Maybe we should laminate the list and carry it in our wallets. Alternatively, we'd like to recommend yet another decision-making model.

Make a Decision With the Help of Four Letters

We are the first to admit that our judgments and gut reactions aren't always the best. (Our wives are the second to admit it, and our children come in a close third.) And while we have found the three methods listed previously to be helpful,

- We aren't really smart enough to understand the Rest Four-Component Test;
- We aren't philosophical enough to contemplate the musing of Aristotle; and
- It takes too long to go through all of Nash's twelve questions (because the decision usually has to be made by the time we get to #6 or #7).

We need a simple question or guideline that will help us think clearly and objectively when we are in an ethical quandary. If you feel the same way, then we have four initials for you that might do the job:

WWJD?

We know what you are thinking (because we used to think it, too). You are skeptical of the whole "What Would Jesus Do?" craze because it seems like a marketing gimmick for T-shirts, caps, bracelets, Bible covers, and boxer shorts. But before you reject the notion of using "WWJD?" as a threshold question for your ethical dilemmas, let us suggest two very good reasons why you might want to give it serious consideration:

Reason #1: It Works!

Isn't that all you really care about? Aren't you looking for something that will help you make better judgments on a consistent basis so that the chart of your character will be in an upward direction rather than a downward, failing trajectory? Well, of all the people who have ever lived, who is the most ethical and moral person you can think of? Jesus has to be at the top of your list. If you want an easy way to double-check your conduct and attitude before you break loose with a response, then asking yourself "What Would Jesus

Do?" is a good way to compare your planned response against a standard that you know is ethically trustworthy.

If you ask yourself the "WWJD?" question before you respond in a certain situation, you'll find that you have a pretty good litmus paper test for whether your planned response is appropriate or needs to be reconsidered. Try it out for a few days. We think you'll be surprised with how effective that simple question can be in giving you a guideline for what you do, say, and think.

Reason #2: It is Biblical!

Asking yourself the "WWJD?" question is not a gimmick. It is a Bible-based principal for living that has been around for centuries.

Moses told the Israelites that they needed to remember God's laws. He told them that they needed to be thinking and talking about God's principles all the time.

> *Hear, O Israel! The Lord is our God, the Lord alone. And you must love the Lord your God will all your heart, all your soul, and all your strength. And you must commit yourselves wholeheartedly to these commands I am giving you today. Repeat them again and again to your children. Talk about them when you are at home and when you are away on a journey, when you are lying down and when you are getting up again ...*
>
> DEUTERONOMY 6:4-7

He didn't say that they should ask, "What Would Jesus Do?" because Jesus hadn't been born yet, but Moses did come up with the idea for a religious bracelet as a reminder to guide your conduct:

> *Tie them to your hands as a reminder, and wear them on your forehead. Write them on the doorposts of your house and on your gates.*
>
> DEUTERONOMY 6:8

The scriptural mandate for use of the "WWJD?" question came from Jesus himself when he said:

> *"I have given you an example to follow. Do as I have done to you."*
>
> JOHN 13:15

If we are supposed to act as Jesus did, then we ought to be asking ourselves what he would do in situations that confront us.

Use of the "WWJD?" question is implied throughout the New Testament by the apostles when they gave instructions to follow Christ's example in passages such as:

- Ephesians 5:1-2: *Follow God's example in everything you do, because you are his dear children. Live a life filled with love for others, following the example of Christ, who loved you and gave himself as a sacrifice to take away your sins.*

- 1 John 2:6: *Those who say they live in God should live their lives as Christ did.*

- Romans 12:2: *Don't copy the behavior and customs of this world, but let God transform you into a new person by changing the way you think. Then you will know what God wants you to do, and you will know how good and pleasing and perfect his will really is.*

Of course, you won't know the answer to the "WWJD?" question if you haven't studied the deeds and character of Christ. But if you are truly interested in strengthening your character—if you really want to change your character failings with a track record of character successes—there is no better way to spend your time.

Your Biggest WWJD? Challenge

If you are going to emulate Jesus, you're going to have to learn to forgive. Forgiving others may be difficult, but forgiving yourself may be the greatest challenge of all. As we discuss in the next chapter, it is not easy, but it is essential if you are going to move from failure to success.

> By not forgiving, I chain myself to a desire to get even, thereby losing my freedom. A forgiven person forgives. This lifelong struggle lies at the heart of the Christian life.

—Henri J.M. Nouwen

CHAPTER 11

Forgiving Failure

For ten chapters we have talked about failure and success from every conceivable angle. Where possible, we have given you real life examples from the pages of Scripture to show you that God loves failures and wants them to succeed. (In Chapter 12 we will show that God is looking for a few more failures.) Now we are going to find out that God has put a condition on our success, and that condition is forgiveness. It's almost as if the road from failure to success goes right through forgiveness. If you try to go around it, you'll never make it to true and lasting success. You may become successful in the eyes of the world, where power and material things are the measure. But you won't be a success in the eyes of God, who measures success by the standards of love and spiritual things.

So let's deal with this eleventh chapter, eleventh hour issue of forgiveness.

We're basically going to look at the two sides of forgiveness, both of which are equally important when it comes to moving from failure to success:

- What it means to be forgiven
- What it means to forgive

What It Means to Be Forgiven

One of the most powerful images we have ever seen is a painting called "Forgiven" by Thomas Blackshear. Color lithographs and prints of this incredible painting are available in Christian stores everywhere, so perhaps you've seen it. If not, we will do our best to describe it to you.

Picture a man dressed in Levis and a t-shirt facing forward. He could be anybody. The man is in the process of collapsing to the ground. His head is tilted to the side and his eyes are closed. On his face is an expression of anguish, but the man doesn't look hopeless. Helpless would be a better description. The man's feet are pulled up in such a way that he would fall to the ground were it not for another man holding him from behind.

The other man, who is also facing forward, but with his head bowed slightly, is dressed in a white robe. Above and behind his head a glow emanates. With powerful arms and hands that bear distinct scars, the second man has reached around the first man from the back in such a way as to prevent him from falling. Indeed, the first man is not supporting himself in any way, but he is holding something in his hands. In his right hand is a large mallet; in his left hand he holds an iron spike. As your eyes follow the two figures to the bottom of the picture, you see a trail of crimson flowing from the feet of the second man. The crimson trail stops in two groups of beautiful white lilies at the bottom corners of the picture.

Underneath this startling image, on the matting surrounding the picture, is the word "Forgiven," and beneath that is this verse from the Bible:

If you, O Lord, kept a record of sins ... who could stand? But with you there is forgiveness; therefore you are feared.

PSALM 130:3-4 NIV

A lot of times a powerful picture is subject to various interpretations. One person sees it one way, and another sees it much differently. With "Forgiven," the reaction from people is always the same. There is no doubt that the first man is everyman. He is you. He is us. Clearly the second man is Jesus, who has forgiven us in spite of our sins—the same sins for which he sacrificed his life. Jesus willingly went to the cross on our behalf, but our sinful natures nailed him there. We deserve to collapse in our sins and die, but Jesus lifts us up because he took the punishment for our sins (see Romans 3:25). In a word, God has forgiven us because of what Jesus did for us.

What a difference between our sin and God's generous gift of forgiveness.
ROMANS 5:15

When You Meet the Artist ...

A few years ago we had the amazing privilege of meeting Thomas Blackshear, the artist who painted "Forgiven." He invited us to his studio, and we saw firsthand the original painting. We were moved beyond words. We asked Thomas how he came to paint "Forgiven." How did he come up with such a powerful statement? Thomas then described to us the remarkable events that led to the painting.

I was at church for a prayer meeting, and I was struggling for an idea for a painting I wanted to paint on the subject of forgiveness. As I prayed with several other men, I shared my burden, and they offered to pray for me. Several of the men laid hands on me as they prayed, and something incredible happened. As I prayed with them with my eyes closed, the image for "Forgiven" came to me in an instant. It wasn't like a part of the image came; I saw the whole thing all at one time. I had never had such an experience before that moment, and I've never had it since.

We reflected on that story as we wrote this chapter, and it suddenly occurred to us that forgiveness comes to us in the same way the image for the painting came to Thomas—all at once. God doesn't piecemeal his forgiveness in sections, like you would give a series of rewards to someone for making improvements. There's nothing we can do to earn God's forgiveness. It is "God's generous gift," and it comes in one package, not in pieces. When we *recognize* who God is, agree that we have fallen short of God's perfect standard, and *decide* by faith to accept God's gift of salvation, we experience God's forgiveness instantly. And the result of all of this is that we are "made right with God" (Romans 3:25).

When we met the gifted artist who painted "Forgiven," we were awestruck for an instant. But when each of us met the Artist who forgave us and freely gives us eternal life, we were changed for eternity. The same thing can happen to you.

You See the Whole Picture

It's so easy to complicate the picture of forgiveness, but it doesn't have to be that way. When you meet the Artist, he shows you the whole picture. God has made forgiveness so clear and simple that we can understand it in an instant. The problem isn't in the understanding of forgiveness. The problem is in the acceptance. Some people just can't accept the fact that God has forgiven them completely, so they put off their decision to accept the free gift of forgiveness. Why does this happen?

Why People Refuse to Accept God's Forgiveness

Back in Chapter 3 we gave you the story of the Prodigal Son as an example for family failure and success. There's another aspect to this parable that Jesus told, and that's forgiveness. Just like the man in the painting is you and us, the Prodigal Son is you and us.

All of us are prodigals. We have all run away from our Father because we think we can do things our own way and make a success of ourselves without his help. When we recognize our bleak condition, we turn away from our rebellion and run back to the Father. And what does he offer us? Unconditional forgiveness. All we have to do is accept it, just as the Prodigal Son did when he said, "Father, I have sinned against both heaven and you" (Luke 15:21).

If we're all prodigals, why don't we all accept God's forgiveness? Henri Nouwen wrote a beautiful book called *The Return of the Prodigal Son*, and in it he made three observations about this human tendency:

1. *We cling to our sins.* "One of the greatest challenges of the spiritual life is to receive God's forgiveness," Nouwen wrote. "There is something in us humans that keeps us clinging to our sins and prevents us from letting God erase our past and offer us a completely new beginning." People are very possessive about their sins, even though they know in their hearts they are wrong. We mistakenly think that if we accept God's unconditional forgiveness, he's going to put unreasonable conditions on our lives and keep us from enjoying ourselves. Of course, the "enjoyment" of sin is temporary, hollow, self-serving, and often destructive, but we don't see it that way, at least not at first.

2. *We think our sins are too great.* There comes a point in our lives when we finally realize that our sins are an offense to God (not to mention the people around us), and we begin to believe that even God is incapable of forgiving all that we have done. Nouwen said: "Sometimes it even seems as though I want to prove to God that my darkness is too great to overcome." Some people believe they don't deserve forgiveness, and of course, they're right. None of us deserves to be forgiven. That's what God's grace is all about. God forgives us because of who Jesus is and what he has done, not because of who we are and what we have done.

3. *We think we can earn our way.* Every religion in the world and every system of belief—except for one—is built on the premise that you can earn your way to heaven. Just do enough good things and don't get into too much trouble, and God will let you in. The only exception to this widely held belief is Christianity, so named because it is based on the person and work of Jesus Christ. "There is no journey to God outside of the journey that Jesus made," wrote Nouwen.

The journey of Jesus went through the cross, and his way is the only way. That's a hard thing for many people to accept. How can there be only one way to God, and why can't I do anything to earn my way? We'd love to give you an easy answer, but all we can tell you is that the forgiveness of God through Christ is a mystery beyond our total comprehension (see 1 Timothy 3:16). But it's the way God designed it. Our only job is to accept it.

The World's Greatest Failure

Henri Nouwen talks about this mystery in the context of the Prodigal Son:

> Jesus himself became the prodigal son for our sake. He left the house of his heavenly Father, came to a foreign country, gave away all that he had, and returned through his cross to his Father's home. All of this he did, not as a rebellious son, but as the obedient son, sent out to bring home all the lost children of God.

From the viewpoint of the religious establishment of his day, Jesus was not exactly "qualified" to forgive sins. He was lowly, homeless, and completely removed from the established religious system. In the eyes of many people—especially the religious leaders—he was a total failure. Worse, in their eyes Jesus was blasphemous, mainly because he had the nerve to say he could forgive sins. "What?" they cried. "This is blasphemy! Who but God can forgive sins!" (Mark 2:5-7).

They were right, of course. No one but God can forgive sins, which is why Jesus was perfectly capable of forgiving sins. This man who was a complete failure in the eyes of the world was in fact God in the flesh (see Philippians 2:6). Not only is he capable of forgiving our sins, he has already done it.

One Solitary Life

He was born in an obscure village, the child of a peasant woman. He grew up in another obscure village, where he worked in a carpenter shop until he was thirty. Then for three years he was an itinerant preacher.

He never had a family or owned a home. He never set foot inside a big city. He never traveled more than two hundred miles from the place he was born. He never wrote a book or held an office. He did none of the things that usually accompany greatness or success.

While he was still a young man, the tide of popular opinion turned against him. His friends deserted him. He was turned over to his enemies and went through the mockery of a trial. He was nailed to a cross between two thieves. While he was dying, his executioners gambled for the only piece of property he had—his coat. When he was dead, he was taken down and laid in a borrowed grave.

Twenty centuries have come and gone, and today he is the central figure for much of the human race. All the armies that ever marched, and all the navies that ever sailed, and all the parliaments that ever sat, and all the kings that ever reigned, put together, have not affected the lives of people upon this earth as powerfully as this "One Solitary Life."

—attributed to James Allan Francis

What It Means to Forgive

Accepting God's forgiveness is hard enough, but here's something that's even harder: forgiving others. When someone offends or wrongs us, often our first response is to resent the offender and hold a grudge. Sometimes we plot ways to get even. But that's the way of the world, not God's way. God asks us to forgive.

C.S. Lewis once said: "Forgiveness is a beautiful word, until you have something to forgive." Isn't that the truth! What a relief it is when someone forgives us. It's like a huge burden has been lifted. But when we are called upon to forgive someone else, we forget all about the grace and mercy we have been shown and we go for revenge. Oh, we think about forgiving, but revenge is so much sweeter.

Jesus told a parable about a guy with an unforgiving heart who also happened to owe the king millions of dollars (see Matthew 18:21-35). The king called in his debtors one day, and the guy with the huge debt pleaded for mercy. The king took mercy on the guy and forgave his debt. So what did the guy do? He went to a fellow debtor who owed him a few thousand dollars and demanded repayment right then and there. When the poor schmuck pleaded for mercy from the creep who had just been forgiven by the king, the creep had him arrested and thrown into jail.

When the king heard about what the arrogant creep had done to the poor schmuck, he was more than a little upset. He hauled El Creepo in and said: "You evil servant! I forgave you that tremendous debt because you pleaded with me. Shouldn't you have mercy on your fellow servant, just as I had mercy on you?" The king then threw the creep into prison until he paid every penny.

As if the moral to the story isn't clear, Jesus tells us anyway:

That's what my heavenly Father will do to you if you refuse to forgive your brothers and sisters in your heart.

MATTHEW 18:35

Ouch! Seems kind of severe. Would God really do that? Why not? He's a just and holy God, not some senile old man who doesn't know what's going on. If you have a heart of unforgiveness, then it's pretty clear you haven't personally taken God's forgiveness to heart, which means you've chosen to go to prison rather than accept God's pardon of forgiveness.

This was a big theme with Jesus. Another time, right after he taught the disciples how to pray, he said:

If you forgive those who sin against you, your heavenly Father will forgive you. But if you refuse to forgive others, your Father will not forgive you.

MATTHEW 5:14-15

At first reading, you might think that God won't forgive you until you forgive others, but that's not what Jesus meant. God has already forgiven us. He sent Jesus into the world to rescue us from sin before we asked for forgiveness and while we were still sinners (see Romans 5:8). What Jesus meant was that we need to realize what forgiveness means before we can accept God's forgiveness. If you can't accept something you don't understand, how can you understand forgiveness if you've never forgiven?

The world says: "Look out for yourself. Don't let anyone take advantage of you." The Bible says: "Be kind to each other, tenderhearted, forgiving one another, just as God through Christ has forgiven you" (Ephesians 4:32).

Forgiving is love's revolution against life's unfairness. When we forgive, we ignore the normal laws that strap us to the natural law of getting even and, by the alchemy of love, we release ourselves from our own painful pasts.

—Lewis B. Smedes

Keep Forgiving

Sometimes forgiving someone one time isn't all that bad. But when you have to forgive the same person a second or a third time—for the same offense—well, that can become very difficult. We want the offender to learn a lesson. How does the old saying go? "Burned once, shame on you; burned twice, shame on me." In other words, I'll forgive you once, you lousy creep. But if you do that again, I won't forgive you a second time. If I do, I'm a fool.

Again, that's the way the world thinks. God has a better idea. And it doesn't involve forgiving two or three times. The standard is a whole lot higher. Jesus told the parable about the unforgiving debtor (we called him El Creepo) in response to a question the apostle Peter asked about forgiveness: "Lord, how often should I forgive someone who sins against me? Seven times?" (Matthew 18:21).

No doubt Peter thought he was being generous with his number seven, but he was way off. "No!" Jesus replied, "seventy times seven!" (Matthew 18:22). Now, people have debated for centuries whether Jesus actually meant that we should forgive someone 490 times, or if he just wanted to make a point. Theoretically, it's possible that you would have to forgive someone 490 times (especially if you're married and have kids), but the real point is that there never should come a time when you aren't willing to forgive someone. If you have trouble grasping that, then look at it this way. How often should God forgive you? Is once enough, or should he cut it off at 490?

Go back a few pages to our story about the "Forgiven" painting. What did the verse at the bottom of the painting say?

If you, O Lord, kept a record of our sins ... who could stand?
PSALM 130:3

If God kept a ledger, none of us could stand. If Jesus wasn't holding us up with his nail-scarred hands, we would collapse in a hopeless heap. But God doesn't keep score. "He has removed our rebellious acts as far away from us as the east is from the west" (Psalm 103:12). When Jesus gave himself as a sacrifice for our sins, it was once and for all.

Now when sins have been forgiven, there is no need to offer any more sacrifices.
HEBREWS 10:18

When it comes to our eternal standing with God, we need to ask for forgiveness only one time. However, when it comes to our *daily walk* with God, we need to go to God and ask forgiveness as often as necessary (and for most of us, that's pretty often). Even as Christians, we have the capacity to sin, and sin puts us into spiritual darkness and breaks our fellowship with God, who is light (see 1 John 1:5). To put it bluntly (Scripture often does this): "We are lying if we say we have fellowship with God but go on living in spiritual darkness" (1 John 1:6). The remedy for this—and the way to get back into fellowship with God—is to confess our sins to God and ask forgiveness, which he will give to us as often as we ask (see 1 John 1:9).

So, if we are to forgive others as God has forgiven us (see Ephesians 4:32), then we need to forgive them as often as it takes.

Vengeance Isn't Yours

The Bible makes it very clear that we aren't supposed to seek revenge when someone else has wronged us. Instead, we are to be reconciled (see Matthew

5:23-24) and turn the other cheek (see Matthew 5:39). "Never avenge yourselves," says the apostle Paul. "Leave that to God" (Romans 12:19).

Vengeance is serious business, better left in the hands of a Professional. By that we don't mean Vinnie the hit man. The only Professional qualified to take vengeance is God, who says: "I will take vengeance; I will repay those who deserve it" (Deuteronomy 32:35). God promises to take care of business, which takes the pressure off of us. Wayne Grudem writes: "In this way whenever we have been wronged, we can give into God's hands any desire to harm or pay back the person who has wronged us, knowing that every wrong in the universe will ultimately be paid for."

How will God do it? According to Grudem, he will repay every wrong in one of two ways:

- either it will turn out to have been paid for by Christ when he died on the cross (if the wrongdoer becomes a Christian);
- or it will be paid for at the final judgment (for those who do not trust in Christ for salvation).

When we are wronged by someone who doesn't know Christ personally, thoughts of revenge and resentment should be the last things in our minds. We should have compassion and pray for that person's salvation. Otherwise he or she will suffer an eternal fate far worse than any vengeful plot we could concoct. It was this attitude that caused Jesus to pray for his executioners: "Father forgive these people, because they don't know what they are doing" (Luke 23:34).

Failing to Forgive Means Failure

The bottom line is that you can get over your failures in every other area we've been talking about in the first ten chapters of this book, but if you fail to forgive others, you will be a failure. There's no other way to say it. As we said in Chapter 4, an unforgiving heart leads to bitterness, anger, and defeat. You need to give it to God and move on. There is a better way to live, and that's the way we want to end this chapter. We want to give you "Twenty-One Principles of Success" as found in Paul's letter to the Romans.

21 Principles of Success
From Romans 12:1-21

1. Set aside your own desires each day and give yourself fully to God (v. 1).
2. Don't act like someone who doesn't know God, and don't conform to the world's values (v. 2).
3. If you want to know what God wants for you, let him change the way you think (v. 2).
4. Don't think too highly of yourself, but don't underestimate yourself either. Be realistic and most of all, measure yourself by God's standards, not the world's (v. 3).
5. Use your God-given abilities and recognize the abilities of others. Realize that you need others as much as they need you (v. 5-8).
6. Stand on the side of good and hate what is wrong in all situations (v. 9).
7. Don't just say you love others, really love them and honor them (v. 9-10).
8. Refuse to be lazy. Serve the Lord with energy and enthusiasm (v. 11).
9. Be amazed and grateful that God has big plans for you (v. 12).
10. When things go upside down, be patient (v. 12).
11. Be a person of prayer. Always (v. 12).
12. When a fellow Christian is in need, offer your help (v. 13).
13. Make your home a place of gracious hospitality (v. 13).
14. Pray for those who criticize or persecute you for being a Christian (v. 14).
15. Be happy for others when they enjoy success. Share their sorrow (v. 15).
16. Do everything you can to get along with others (v. 16, 18).
17. Never think you are better than anybody else, and never think you know it all (v. 16).
18. If someone wrongs you, don't try to get even. Leave it to God (v. 17, 19).
19. Others should be able to see that you are a person of honor in everything you do (v. 17).
20. Treat your enemies with kindness (v. 20).
21. Never let evil get the best of you. Conquer evil by doing good (v. 21).

> We are all faced with a series of great opportunities
> brilliantly disguised as overwhelming problems.

—Howard Hendricks

CHAPTER 12

God Is Looking for a
Few Good Failures

C ongratulations! You are about to accomplish something few people do
these days, with all the distractions and time pressures and all. You are
about to finish a book. OK, we admit, this isn't like running a marathon or
winning an election or anything really big like that, but don't kid yourself.
Finishing a book isn't all that easy. The fact that you're reading this last chapter means you are a person of persistence. It also means that you understand
(if you've been taking notes) something very important: failure is not fatal.

If you haven't been taking notes or underlining or using a highlighter,
relax. We've got you covered. As a public service to you, the reader, we have
selected one key nugget from each chapter. Think of this as a convenient
way to review the book (even though there won't be a test at the end). Here
they are, twelve things to remember:

Failing doesn't make you a failure.
Failing gives you an opportunity
to learn from your mistakes.

* * *

The greatest accomplishments come from people
who are afraid to fail.

* * *

In failing families, everyone marches to the beat of a
different drummer. In successful families, everyone
plays a different instrument, but they march together.

* * *

The way to keep your relationships from failing is to
help others succeed.

* * *

Your best chance at finding true love is first to find
love from the One who is true.

* * *

Failure comes when you refuse to invite God to be the
Senior Partner in the work he has called you to do.

* * *

No one plans to fail. They just fail to plan.

* * *

Making good decisions is not about avoiding failure.
It's about building success.

* * *

God has been faithful in the past, he is faithful to you
right now, and he promises to be faithful in the future.

* * *

A person of character does the right thing
even in the minor, insignificant details of life.

* * *

The path from failure to success
runs through forgiveness.

* * *

God is looking for a few good failures.

* * *

This last nugget brings us to the topic at hand. This is the concept we want to leave you with. It's pointless to avoid failure. For one thing, you'll never succeed at it, and for another, the only people God uses are failures. To put it another way, if you don't fail, God won't use you. Simple as that. Remember that great quote from Chuck Swindoll earlier in the book? It's worth repeating:

"Our problem isn't that we've failed. Our problem is that we haven't failed enough. We haven't been brought low enough to learn what God wants us to learn."

This doesn't mean that you should deliberately put yourself in situations where you know you will fail, just so God can teach you something. That would be really dumb, like taking poison just so you can test the antidote. To the best of your ability, you need to put yourself in positions where you can succeed. But you must realize that failure is going to happen despite your best efforts. You're going to flunk a test, goof up a report, lose a client, or say the wrong thing, even though you didn't deliberately decide to fail. It's going to hurt, but you can't let your failure get you down, because you are now in a place where God can use you.

You're also going to fail because you didn't put out any effort at all, or worse, because you did exactly the opposite of what you should have done. You will lie when you should be truthful, say something unkind about someone behind his or her back, or overlook an opportunity to help someone in need. There's only one way to deal with your failure. You need to recognize your mistake, confess your sin, and accept God's forgiveness. It's going to hurt, but don't let your failure get you down, because you are now in a place where God can use you.

There are those times when you are a victim of circumstances beyond your control. You will get depressed, face an illness, get in an accident, or get the boot in a relationship. You're not exactly living a life of success. It's going to hurt, but don't give up hope, because you are now in a place where God can use you.

The Failure Hall of Fame

Throughout the book we have explored the lives of several people in the Bible who God used in powerful ways. In every case, these people failed in some way or another. Yet it was at the point of their failure when God used them in ways no one could predict.

- *Adam and Eve* disobeyed God and brought sin and death upon the entire human race (that would have to rank pretty high on the list of Top Ten Failures of All Time). Yet God used their failure to introduce his plan of salvation through Jesus Christ (see Romans 5:18).

- *Moses* committed murder and hid out in the wilderness. Yet God used him to lead his people out of slavery (see Exodus 3:10).

- *Abigail* had a jerk for a husband, yet she loved him anyway, and God provided for her (see 1 Samuel 25:24, 33).

- *David* made a series of bad decisions that cost people their lives and almost brought down his kingdom, yet the Lord forgave him when David confessed his sin (see 2 Samuel 12:13).

- *Elijah* got depressed and wallowed in his own pity. This is where God strengthened Elijah and cared for him (see 1 Kings 19:4, 7, 12).

- *The Prodigal Son* squandered his inheritance and lived with the pigs, yet his father took him back and restored his position when the Prodigal Son confessed his sin (see Luke 15:21-22).

- Though he was God, *Jesus* took the position of a servant and died a criminal's death. Because of this, "God raised him to the heights of heaven and gave him a name that is above every name" (see Philippians 2:6-9).

- *Peter* was still useful to God after denying Christ. There is no reason why you should assume that your character failings are fatal (see John 21:15-22.).

- *Paul* struggled with sin even though he knew better. Yet through Jesus Christ he could claim victory over sin (see Romans 7:24-25).

Do you see the pattern here? Every person God uses is a failure. To put it another way, God uses failures to accomplish what he wants done. Rather than being discouraged by those times when you fail, see them as opportunities. Rather than living your life under the fear of failure, go through each day with the confidence of Romans 8:28:

"And we know that God causes everything to work together for the good of those who love God and are called according to his purpose for them."

A Balanced View of Failure

Noted theologian Larry Richards has studied the patterns of failure in the lives of Bible characters. Here are his suggestions for keeping a balanced view of failure:

Even those with great faith can fail. Let's not be shocked at our own or at others' weaknesses. The apostle Peter emphatically told Jesus that he would never forsake him, yet he failed miserably—not once, but three times! Never think you are too good to fail.

Personal failures affect others. What we do and are always has its impact on those around us. King David was a very public person, so his personal failure had great repercussions for the people around him. Don't ever think your failure impacts you alone.

Only God can redeem our failures. Never let guilt or shame turn you away from God. He is the only One who can help. Adam and Eve tried to hide from God after they had sinned. They felt their guilt and were ashamed. But they had nowhere else to go. Only God could help them, and he was willing to do so.

God does not abandon us when our weaknesses betray us. God can and will intervene for us when we turn to him. By all rights, the father of the Prodigal Son could have punished his son for his foolish behavior. But he forgave his son and restored him to a place of honor, even when the older brother objected.

God's View of Failure

One of the hardest things to do in life is to see things from God's viewpoint. On the one hand we need to see sin as something that God hates. We need to realize that God cannot have fellowship with someone who is living in the darkness of sin (see 1 John 1:6). On the other hand, we need to see failure from God's perspective. In his book, *Redeeming Failure*, Michael M. Smith writes that God's view of failure has four components:

- *He expects it.* God isn't a cynic, but a realist. God knows you so well that every hair on your head is numbered (which is fewer for Stan than for Bruce). Our failures don't surprise God, because "he understands how weak we are" (Psalm 103:14).

- *He forgives it.* We've been through this, but it's worth repeating: there's nothing you can do that God can't forgive. Even more impressive, "He has not punished us for all our sins, nor does he deal with us as we deserve" (Psalm 103:10).

- *He uses it.* God is a master of taking something weak and useless and using it for his purposes and glory. The apostle Paul had a "thorn" in his flesh. No one knows for sure what it was, but it probably made Paul feel like a failure. When he asked the Lord to take it away, here's what Jesus said: "My power works best in your weakness" (2 Corinthians 12:9).

- *He sees past it.* Here's a news flash: God is not discouraged, disheartened, or disillusioned by your failures. When you read in the Bible about God and how he operates, you see that he is the first one who wants to move on and start fresh. He will do the same for you.

Listen to God's Voice

Do you ever wish you could hear God speak to you? Wouldn't it be great to hear God talk like a wise and loving father, so there would be no question about what you should do next? Well, you can hear God's voice—not in an audible way, like he spoke to Adam and Eve, Noah, and Moses—but in a way that's loud and clear. The problem is that you aren't always listening.

When you listen to someone, you have to focus. Let's say you're at a party in a roomful of people. Everyone is talking, plus there's music playing, and a bunch of people are playing video games. You see a very special person you haven't talked to in a while, so you walk over to start a conversation. The special person sits down with you and begins to talk. There's noise and static all around you, but you really want to hear what this person has to say, so you listen intently. You concentrate on the person. You focus. It takes some effort, but you can do it, and the more you tune into the conversation, the easier it becomes.

Suddenly, without realizing it, the other voices and noise fade into the background, and the special person's voice gets clearer and more distinct. You may be in a crowd of people, but as far as you are concerned, it's just the two of you.

That's the way it is with God's voice. He is speaking, but he's not shouting. There are other voices out there—they could be people or pressures or temptations or your own failures—calling out for your attention, and they can easily drown out God's voice. That's why we have to focus on God and really listen. Remember Elijah's pity party? God spoke to Elijah when he was feeling like a complete failure. The way God did it is a lesson for all of us.

Elijah was expecting God to put on a big production. Elijah experienced a windstorm, an earthquake, and a fire, but God wasn't in any of them. Elijah tried to hear God, he was doing his best to experience God, but he wasn't listening to God. When Elijah finally listened, God came to him in a "gentle whisper" (1 Kings 19:12). And when Elijah finally heard God's voice, he knew what he was supposed to do next.

We're no different from Elijah. We have all this stuff going on around us. We find ourselves in the middle of a crisis. We get into trouble. We experience failure. The wind is blowing, the earth is shaking, and we're feeling the heat. Desperately, we're looking for God to shout through the static and give us direction, and all the while God is right there, quietly speaking to us through the still small voice of the Holy Spirit. "Be silent and know that I am God," he says to us (Psalm 46:10).

Our tendency is to thrash around and struggle to see God in the fury of our lives, but that's not the way he works. He's there, but he's waiting for us to step back, take a deep breath, and listen. "The majority of us cannot hear anything but ourselves," Oswald Chambers wrote. "And we cannot hear anything God says. But to be brought to the place where we can hear the call of God is to be profoundly changed."

When you finally hear the voice of God—often after you've failed in some way—it does change you, because God is in the business of changing those he loves into something better. If you have come into a relationship with God through Jesus Christ by faith, your spiritual condition has already been changed (see 2 Corinthians 5:17). But God isn't finished with you. He wants to keep changing you so you can be more like him.

And as the Spirit of the Lord works within us, we become more and more like him and reflect his glory even more.

2 CORINTHIANS 3:18

That's the wonderful and sometimes confusing thing about the Christian life. God expects our failure, he forgives our failure, he uses our failure, and he sees past our failure. We may not always see what God is doing, but we can always be confident that God knows what he is doing. Our job isn't to figure it out, but to trust God for the end result. And there's only one way to do this.

We do this by keeping our eyes on Jesus, on whom our faith depends from start to finish.

HEBREWS 12:2

God Is Looking for a Few Good Failures

There's a great verse tucked away in 2 Chronicles (that's the place in your Bible where the pages are still stuck together). Check this out:

The eyes of the Lord search the whole earth in order to strengthen those whose hearts are fully committed to him.

2 CHRONICLES 16:9

God is also looking for those who know what it's like to fail. Our hearts become fully committed to God when we understand that only he can turn our failures into success. God is the world's greatest recruiter, and he's looking for failures willing to do his work. The great prophet Isaiah understood this when he was at his lowest point. He realized how pitiful he really was, but more importantly, he understood how wonderful God is. Here's what Isaiah said:

> *My destruction is sealed, for I am a sinful man and a member of a sinful race. Yet I have seen the King, the Lord Almighty!*
>
> ISAIAH 6:5

Then God did something truly amazing. He expected, forgave, used, and looked past Isaiah's failure and gave him the greatest challenge of all:

> *"Whom should I send as a messenger to my people? Who will go for us?"*

And Isaiah answered back:

> *"Lord, I'll go! Send me."*

God's challenge wasn't just for Isaiah. He is asking all of us the same question: "Who will tell others about me?" God wants to know who among us will be bold enough to deliver the message of hope in a world of failure. He's asking the question in a gentle whisper, and he's waiting to find out who is really listening.

Bibliography

Arnold, John D., and Bert Tompkins. *How to Make the Right Decisions.* New York: Ballantine Books, 1982.

Ashcroft, John. *Lessons From a Father to His Son.* Nashville, Tenn.: Thomas Nelson, 1998.

Bennis, Warren, and Burt Nanus. *Leaders.* New York: Harper & Row, 1986.

Blackaby, Henry T., and Claude V. King. *Experiencing God.* Nashville, Tenn.: Broadman & Holman Publishers, 1994.

Cook, William H. *Success, Motivation, and the Scriptures.* Nashville, Tenn.: Broadman Press, 1974.

Covey, Stephen R. *The Seven Habits of Highly Effective People.* New York, Simon & Schuster, 1990.

Friesen, Garry. *Decision Making and the Will of God.* Sisters, Ore.: Multnomah, 1980.

Galloway, Dale. *Dare to Discipline Yourself.* Old Tappan, N.J.: Fleming H. Revell, 1984.

Getz, Gene A. *The Measure of a Family.* Ventura, Calif.: Regal, 1976.

Graves, Stephen R., and Thomas G. Addington. *The Fourth Frontier: Exploring the New World of Work.* Nashville, Tenn.: Word, 2000.

Grudem, Wayne. *Systematic Theology.* Grand Rapids, Mich.: Zondervan, 1994.

Hybels, Bill. *Christians in the Marketplace.* Wheaton, Ill.: Victor, 1991.

Hybels, Bill. *Making Life Work: Putting God's Wisdom into Action.* Downers Grove, Ill.: InterVarsity, 1998.

Jeffers, Susan. *Feel the Fear and Do It Anyway.* New York: Fawcett Columbine, 1987.

Komives, Susan R., Nance Lucas and Timothy R. McMahon. *Exploring Leadership: For College Students Who Want to Make a Difference.* San Francisco: Jossey-Bass, 1998.

Lutzer, Erwin W. *Failure: The Backdoor to Success.* Chicago: Moody, 1975.

Maxwell, John. *Becoming a Person of Influence.* Nashville, Tenn.: Thomas Nelson, 1997.

Maxwell, John. *Failing Forward.* Nashville, Tenn.: Thomas Nelson, 2000.

McClung, Floyd, Jr. *God's Man in the Family.* London, England.: Kingsway, 1994.

McGinnis, Alan Loy. *The Friendship Factor.* Minneapolis: Augsburg, 1979.

Nieder, John and Thompson, Thomas. *Forgive and Love Again.* Eugene, Oreg.: Harvest House, 1991.

Nouwen, Henri. *The Return of the Prodigal Son.* New York: Doubleday, 1992.

Novak, Michael. *Business as a Calling.* New York: Free Press, 1996.

Ortberg, John. *The Life You've Always Wanted.* Grand Rapids, Mich.: Zondervan, 1997.

Peretti, Frank. *The Wounded Spirit.* Nashville, Tenn.: Word, 2000.

Richards, Lawrence O. *The 365 Day Devotional Commentary.* Wheaton, Ill.: Victor, 1990.

Rinehart, Stacy T. *Upside Down: The Paradox of Servant Leadership.* Colorado Springs, Colo.: NavPress, 1998.

Sanders, J. Oswald. *Spiritual Leadership.* Chicago, Ill.: Moody, 1994.

Schuller, Robert. *You Can Become the Person You Want to Be.* Old Tappen, N.J.: Fleming H. Revell, 1973.

Smith, Fred. *You and Your Network.* Mechanicsburg, Penn.: Executive Books, 1998.

Smith, Michael M. *Redeeming Failure.* Colorado Springs, Colo.: NavPress, 1999.

Swindoll, Charles R. *David.* Nashville, Tenn.: Word, 1997.

Swindoll, Charles R. *Elijah.* Nashville, Tenn.: Word, 2000.

Swindoll, Charles R. *Esther.* Nashville, Tenn.: Word, 1997.

Swindoll, Charles R. *Moses.* Nashville, Tenn.: Word, 1999.

Wolgemuth, Robert. *Daddy @ Work.* Grand Rapids, Mich.: Zondervan, 1999.

Yancey, Philip. *Reaching for the Invisible God.* Grand Rapids, Mich.: Zondervan, 2000.

Ziglar, Zig. *Success for Dummies.* Foster City, Calif.: IDG Books Worldwide, 1998.